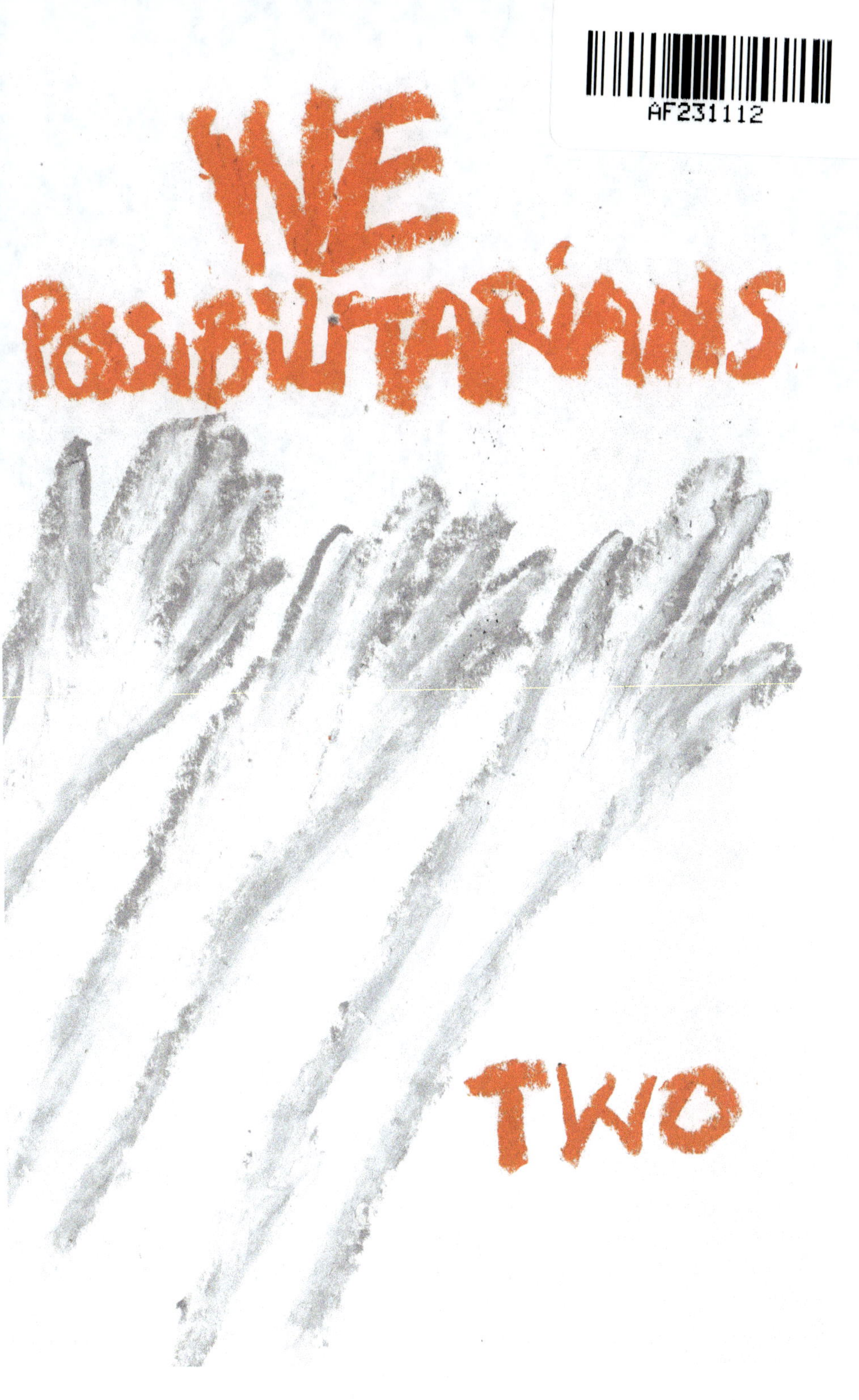

WE
POSSIBILITARIANS
TWO
AF231112

ISBN-13: 978-1-959984-50-4

Library of Congress Number: 2024940704

07-18-2024

WE ARE AT THE BEGINNING OF
THE POSSIBILITARIAN TAKEOVER OF
SOCIETY. WE HEREWITH DISPOSE OF
THE INCOMPETENT RULING CLASS BY
UNDERTHROWING IT FROM THE TOES
UP, & WE IMMEDIATELY IMPLEMENT
THE 1000 ALTERNATIVES TO THE
DESTRUCTIVE HABITS OF CAPITALISM.

POLITICS MUST ABANDON ITS
TRADITIONAL WAR & WEAPONS
PREOCCUPATIONS & MAKE THE
SEVERE HEALTH ISSUES OF OUR ONE
AND ONLY MOTHER EARTH AND HER
EARTHLINGS ITS PRIMARY CONCERN.

THE TERM "POSSIBILITARIAN"
APPROXIMATES THE WORD
"MÖGLICHKEITSMENSCH" IN ROBERT
MUSIL'S NOVEL, "THE MAN WITHOUT
QUALITIES", & HAS BEEN WIDELY USED IN
BREAD & PUPPET PRODUCTIONS.

POSSIBILITARIAN

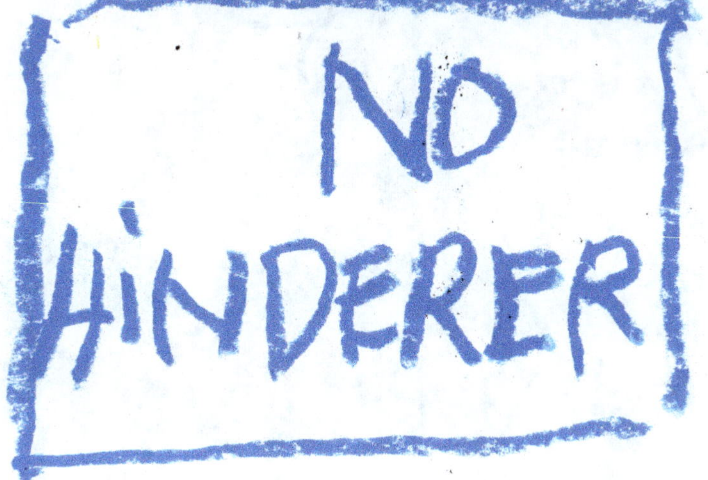

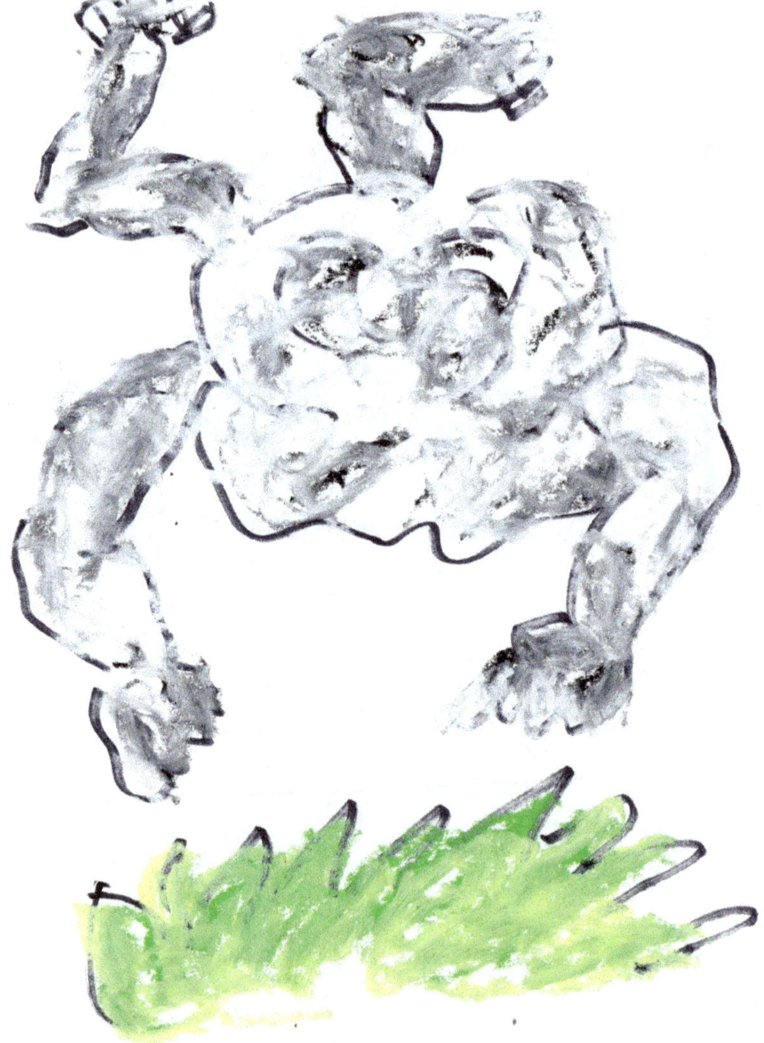

OUR MIND'S
MUSCLES TOO
OFTEN UNEMPLOYED

+ NOT APPLIED TO

THE SORROW + NEED THAT
SURROUND US

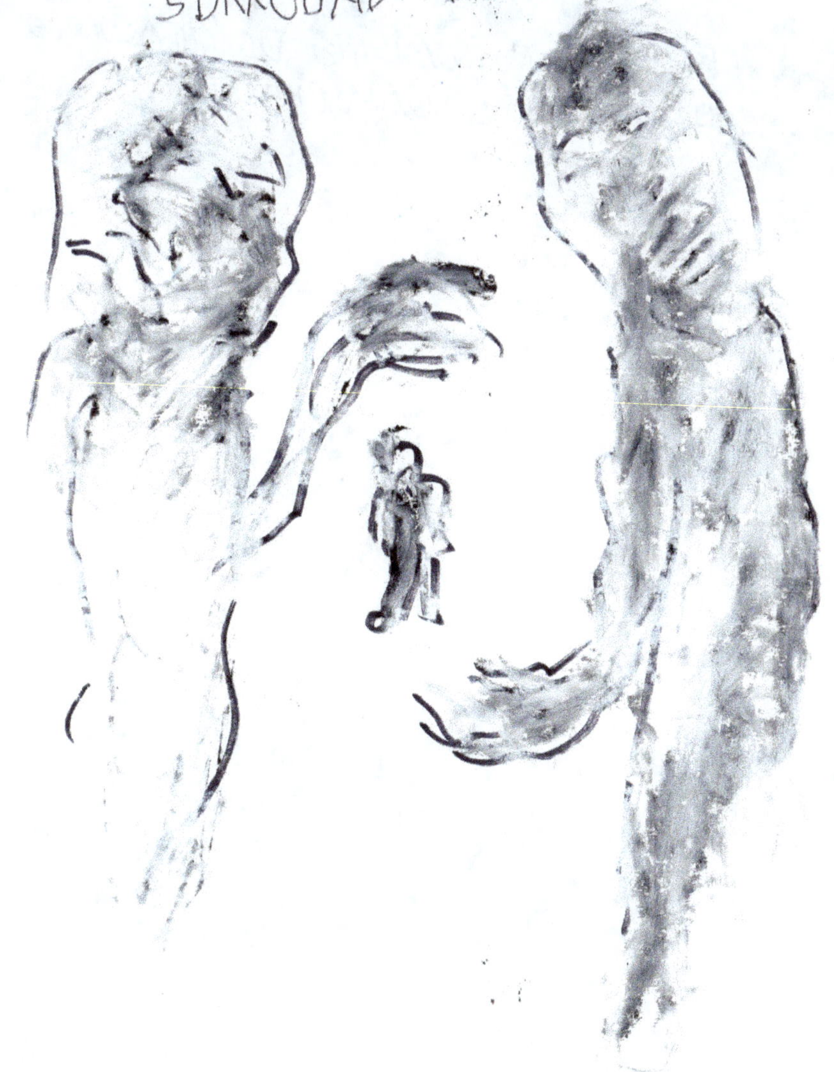

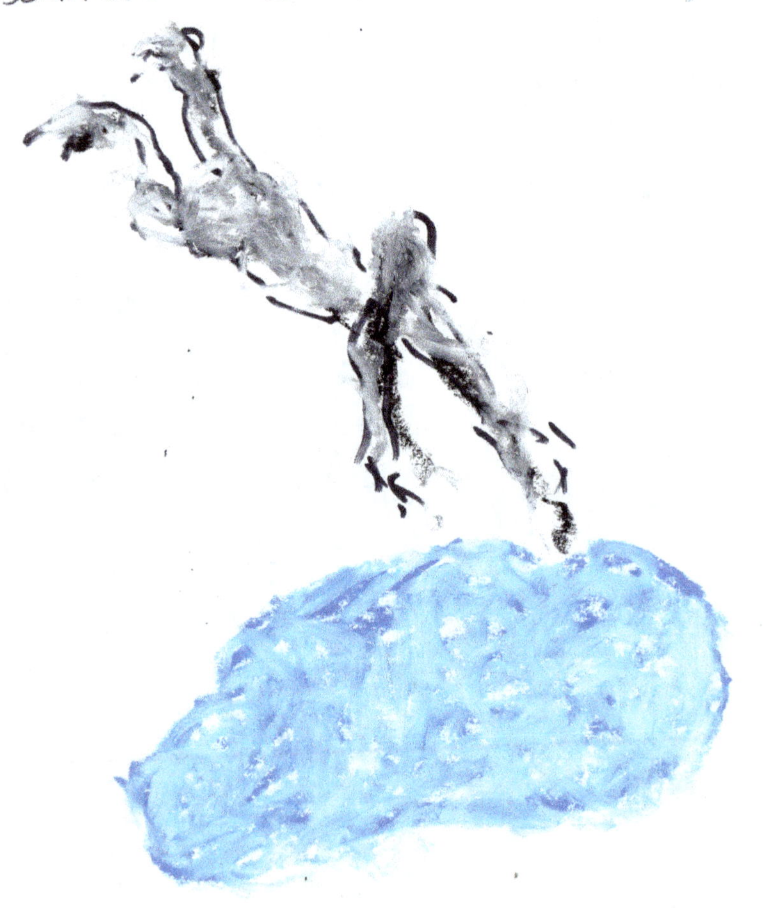

DID WE SUCCEED
TO JUMP INTO THE POOL
OF THIS DAY'S
FRESH AIR PROMISING US MIRACULOUS
SOLUTIONS TO GODDAM PROBLEMS ?

DID WE JUMP over

THE PILE OF FRESH SHIT THAT THE LAST DAY PUT IN OUR WAY?

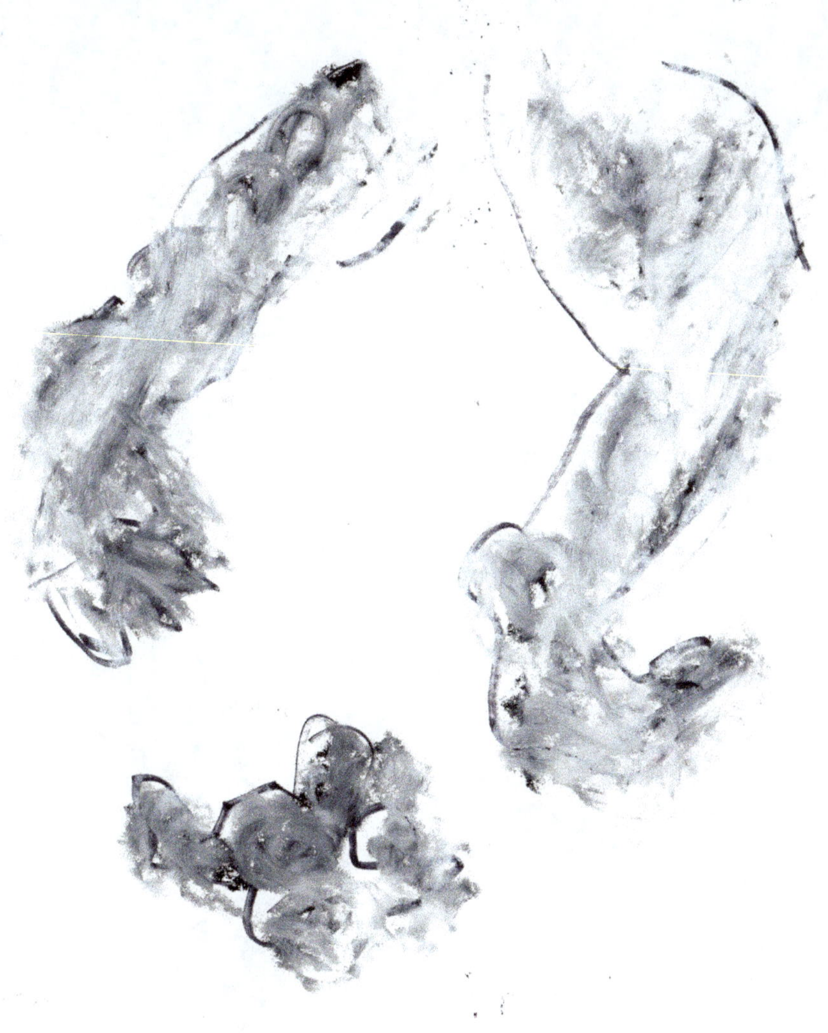

DID THE YOUNG

BLOSSOMING GODS WHO MEANT TO VISIT
MATERIALIZE?

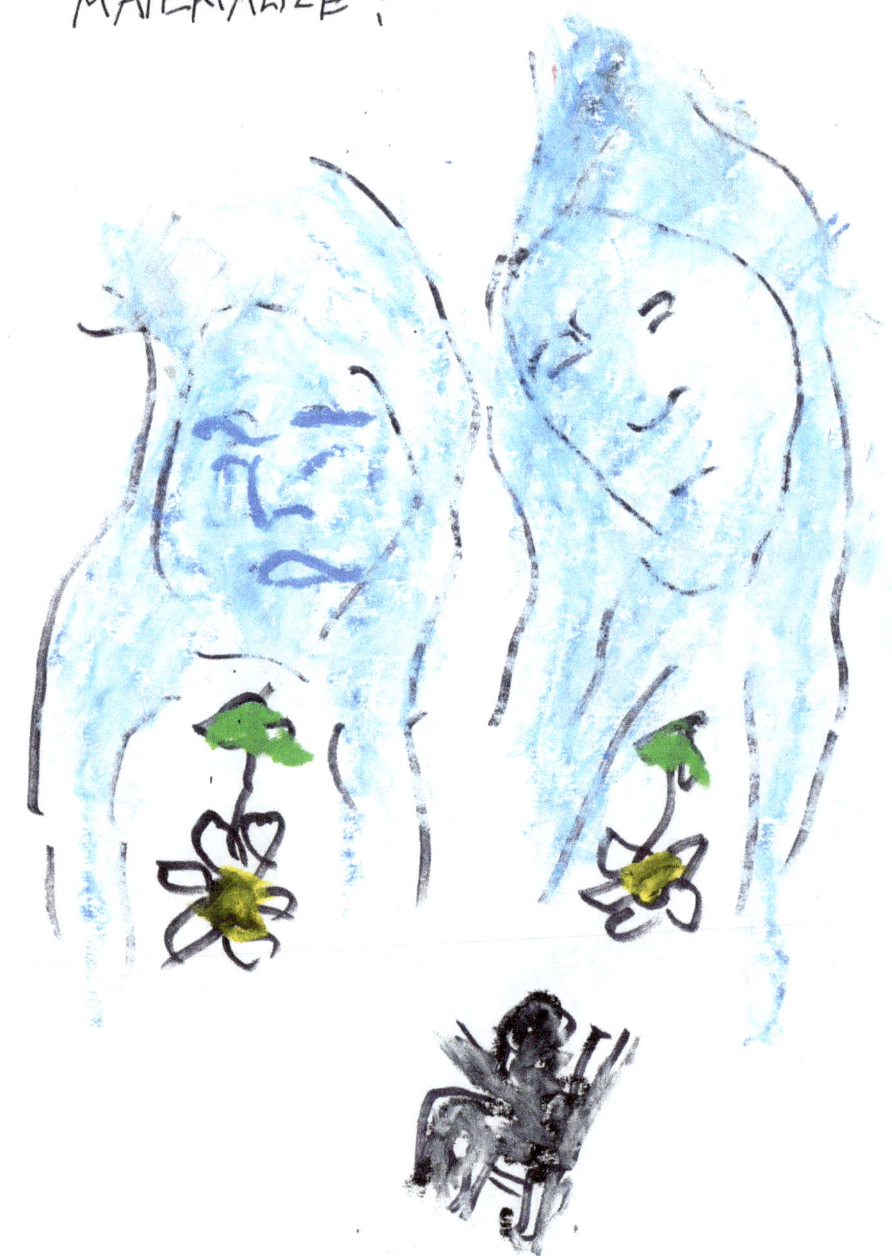

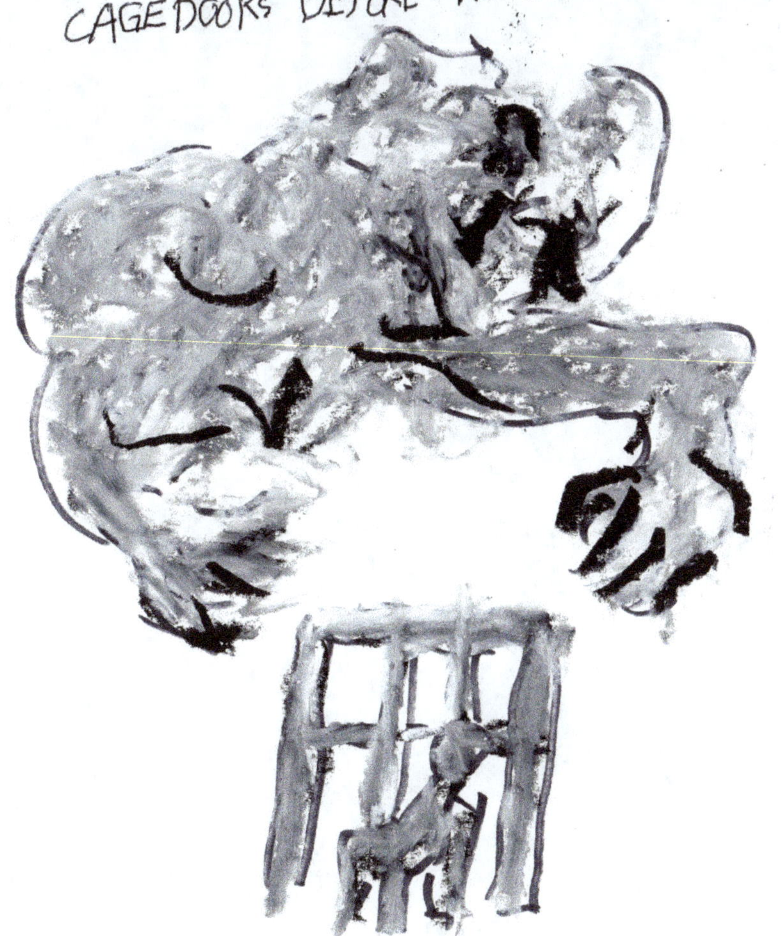

+ AS THE HINDERER
HINDERS US + REINFORCES THE
CAGEDOORS BEFORE WE SUCCEED TO EXIT

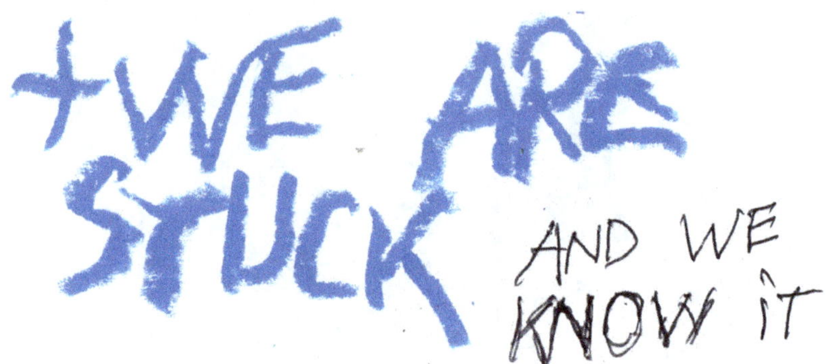

WE ARE STUCK
AND WE KNOW IT

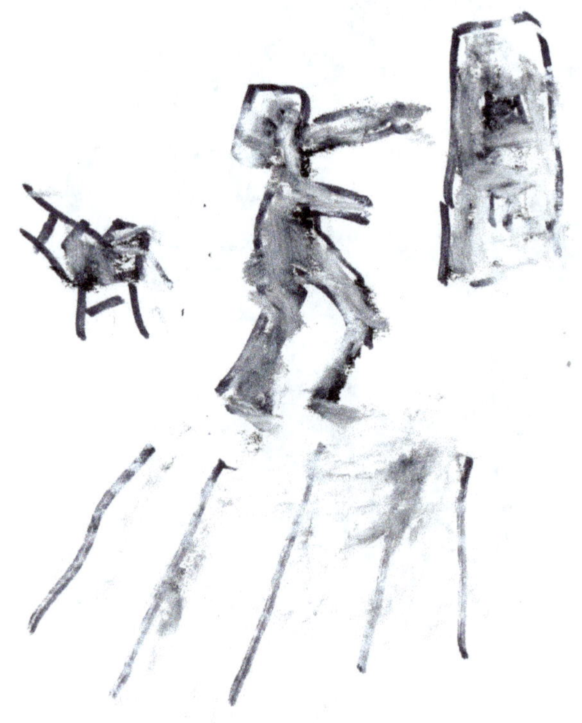

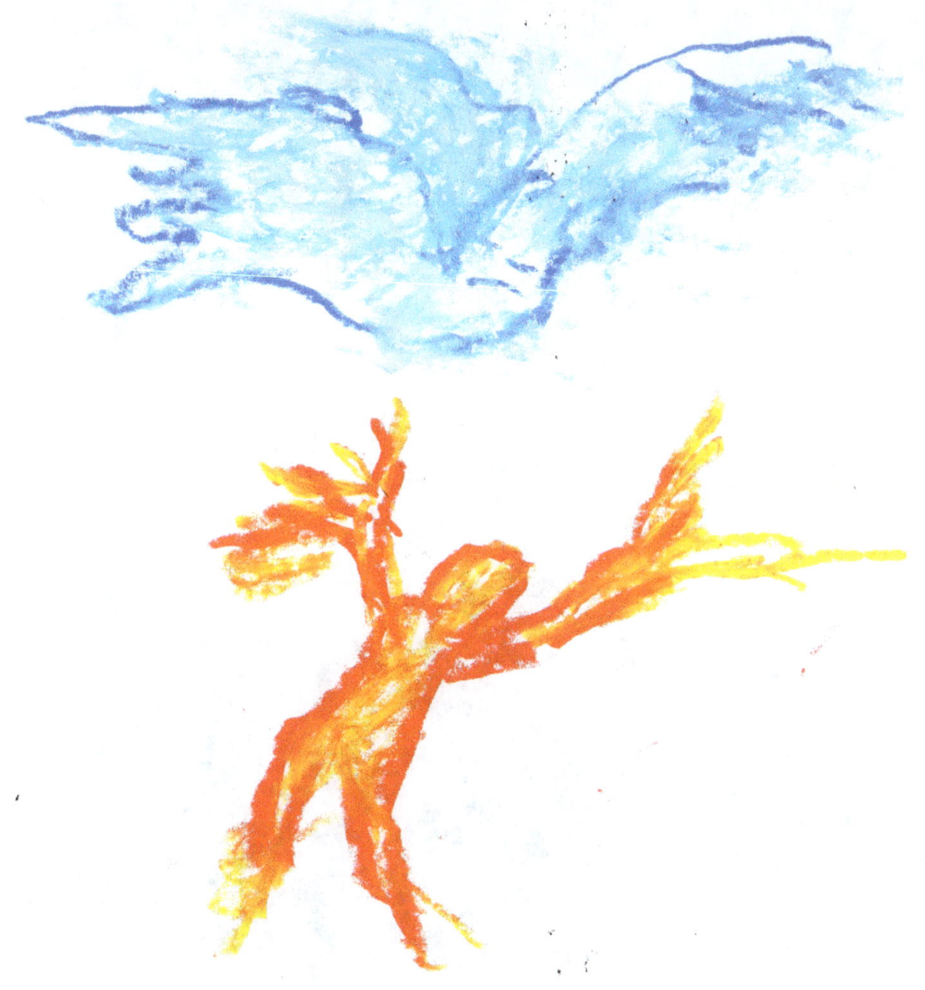

YOUR SWEET DREAM
OF FLYING SUBLIMELY ABOVE IT ALL
TURNS INTO A NIGHTMARE

I KNOW FULL WELL

THE HINDERER WHO PREVENTED THE
GODS' VISITING + BLOSSOMING IS NOT
OUTSIDE BUT ↓

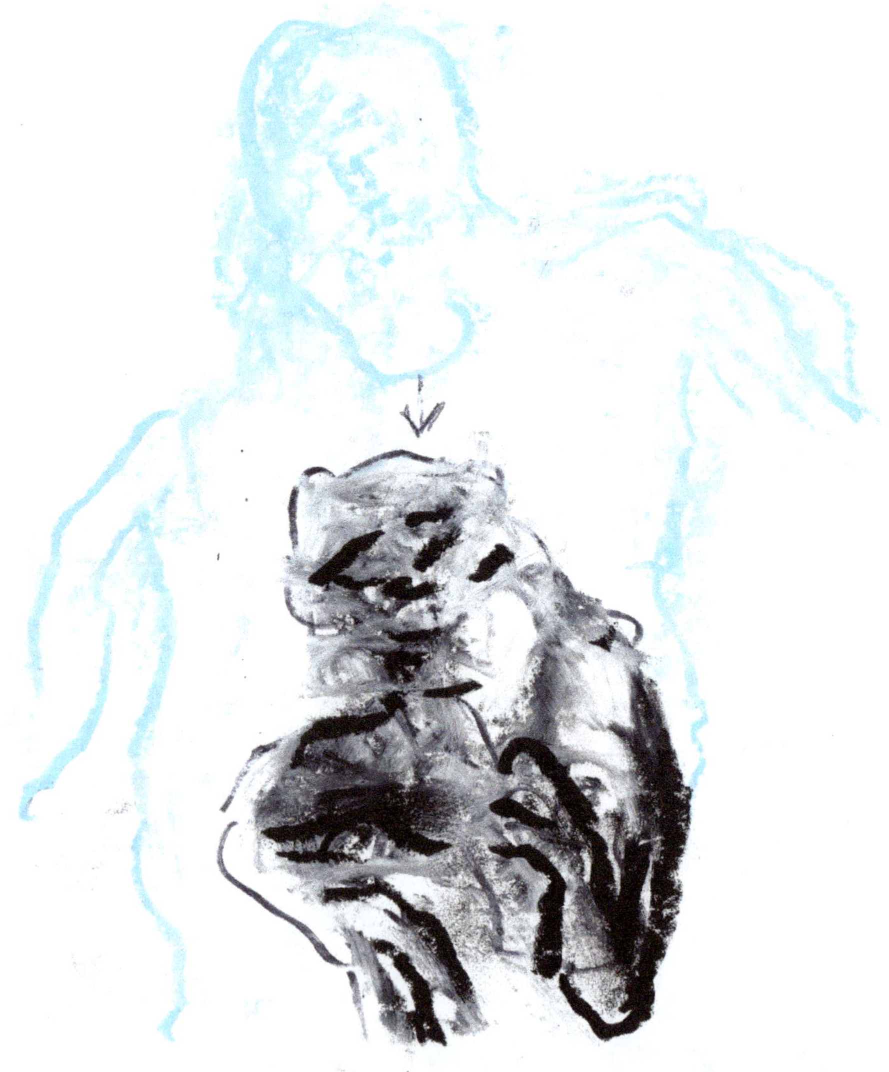

+ THE GODS WILL VISIT

+ BLOSSOM

POSSIBILITARIAN

TRUTH
+
TRUTH INDUSTRY

TRUTH iNDUSTRY

SPECIALIZING iN
½ TRUTH
¼ TRUTH
UPSIDEDOWN TRUTH
+ OMISSION OF TRUTH

OUR ADMIRATION TO YOU THE TRUTHTELLERS

WHO SACRIFICED THEIR + OFTEN THEIR FAMILIES' LIVES TO SPEAK THE PLAIN TRUTH INTO THE FACE OF THE TRUTHMURDERERS

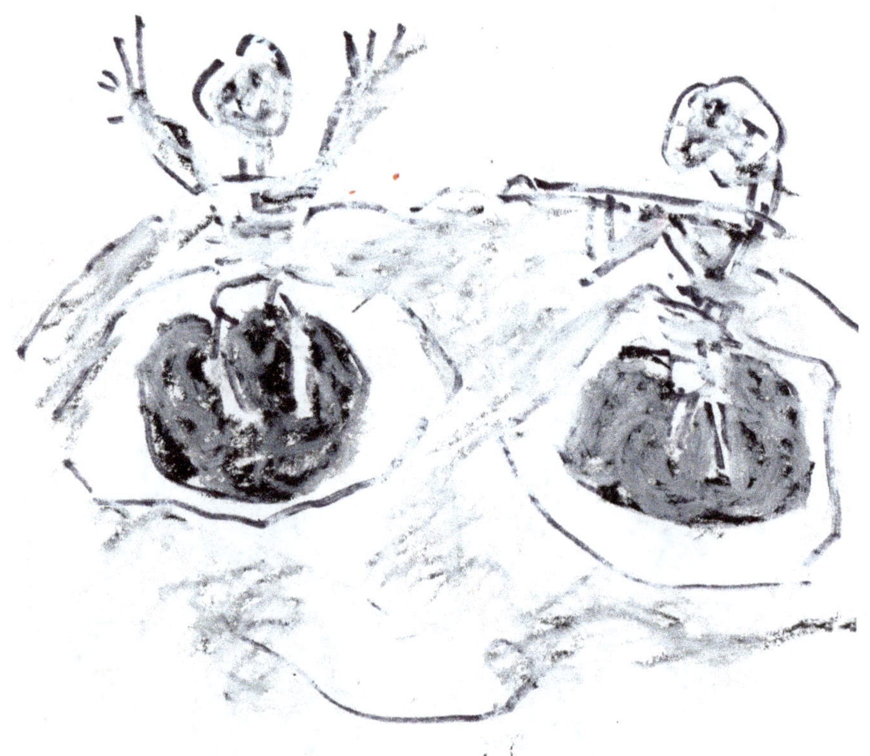

October 7, 2023
Shai Regev
Ayelet Arnin
Yaniv Zohar
Mohammad Al-Salhi
Mohammad Jarghoun
Ibrahim Mohammad Lafi

October 8, 2023
Assaad Shamlakh

October 10, 2023
Saeed al-Taweel
Mohammed Sobh
Hisham Alnwajha

October 11, 2023
Mohamed Fayez Abu Matar

October 12, 2023
Ahmed Shehab

October 13, 2023
Salam Mema
Husam Mubarak
Issam Abdallah

October 14, 2023
Yousef Maher Dawas

October 16, 2023
Abdulhadi Habib

October 17, 2023
Mohammad Balousha
Issam Bhar

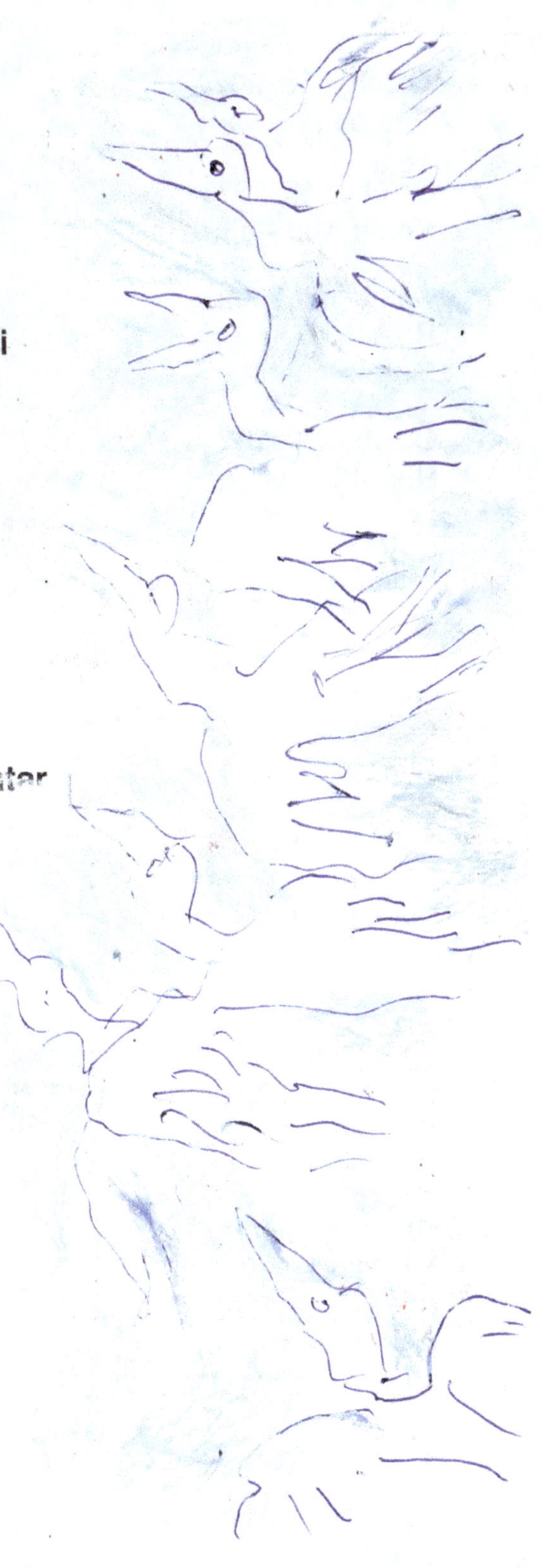

October 18, 2023
Sameeh Al-Nady

October 19, 2023
Khalil Abu Aathra

October 20, 2023
Roee Idan
Mohammed Ali

October 22, 2023
Roshdi Sarraj

October 23, 2023
Mohammed Imad Labad

October 25, 2023
Jamal Al-Faqaawi
Saed Al-Halabi
Ahmed Abu Mhadi
Salma Mkhaimer

October 26, 2023
Duaa Sharaf

October 27, 2023
Yasser Abu Namouss

October 30, 2023
Nazmi Al-Nadim

October 31, 2023
Imad Al-Wahidi
Majed Kashko

November 1, 2023
Majd Fadl Arandass
Iyad Matar
Ivawad

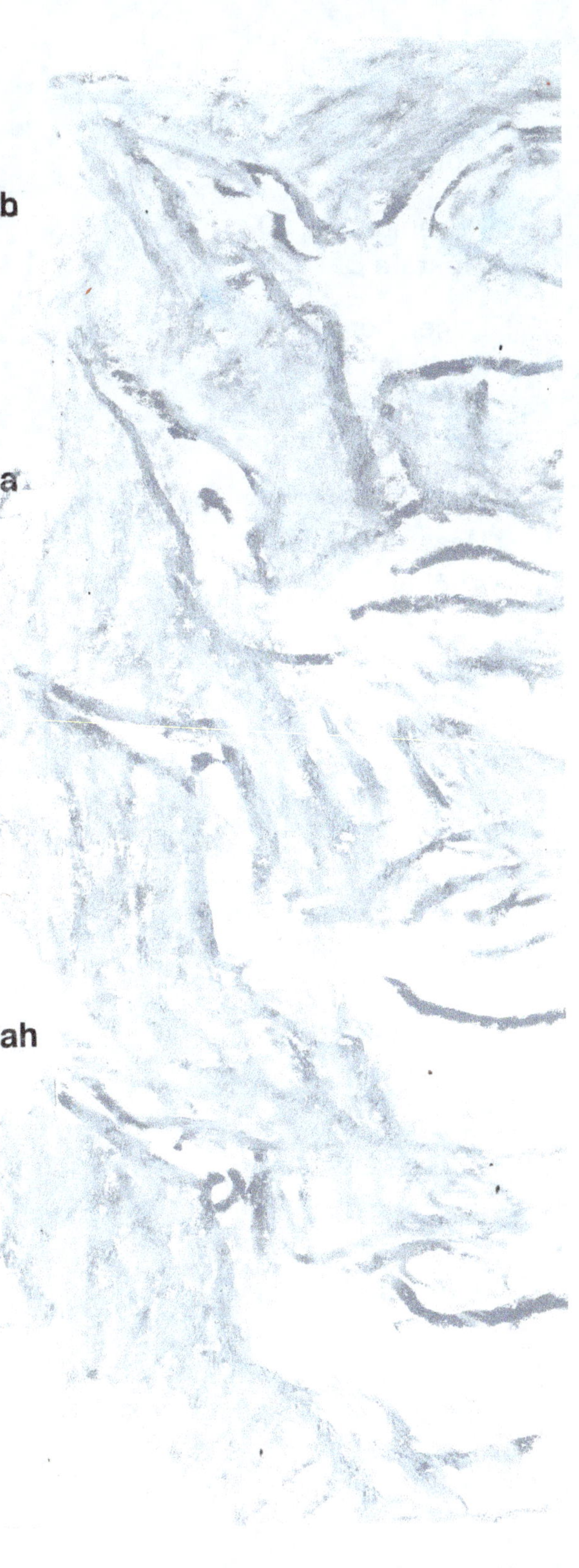

November 2, 2023
Mohamad Al-Bayyari
Mohammed Abu Hatab

November 5, 2023
Mohamed Al Jaja

November 7, 2023
Yahya Abu Manih
Mohamed Abu Hassira

November 10, 20232
Ahmed Al-Qara

November 13, 2023
Ahmed Fatima
Yaacoub Al-Barsh

November 18, 2023
Abdelhalim Awad
Sari Mansour
Hassouneh Salim
Mostafa El Sawaf
Amro Salah Abu Hayah
Mossab Ashour

November 19, 2023
Bilal Jadallah

November 20, 2023
Ayat Khadoura

November 21, 2023
Farah Omar
Rabih Al Maamari
November 22, 2023

November 23, 2023
Mohamed Mouin Ayyash

November 24, 2023
Mostafa Bakeer

December 1, 2023
Abdullah Darwish
Montaser Al-Sawaf
Adham Hassouna

December 3, 2023
Hassan Farajallah
Shaima El-Gazzar

December 9, 2023
Duaa Jabbour
Ola Atallah

December 15, 2023
Samer Abu Daqqa

December 17, 2023
Assem Kamal Moussaa
Haneen Kashtan

December 18, 2023
Abdallah Alwan

December 19, 2023
Adel Zorob

December 22, 2023
Mohamed Khalifeh

December 23, 2023
Mohamed Naser Abu Huwaidi

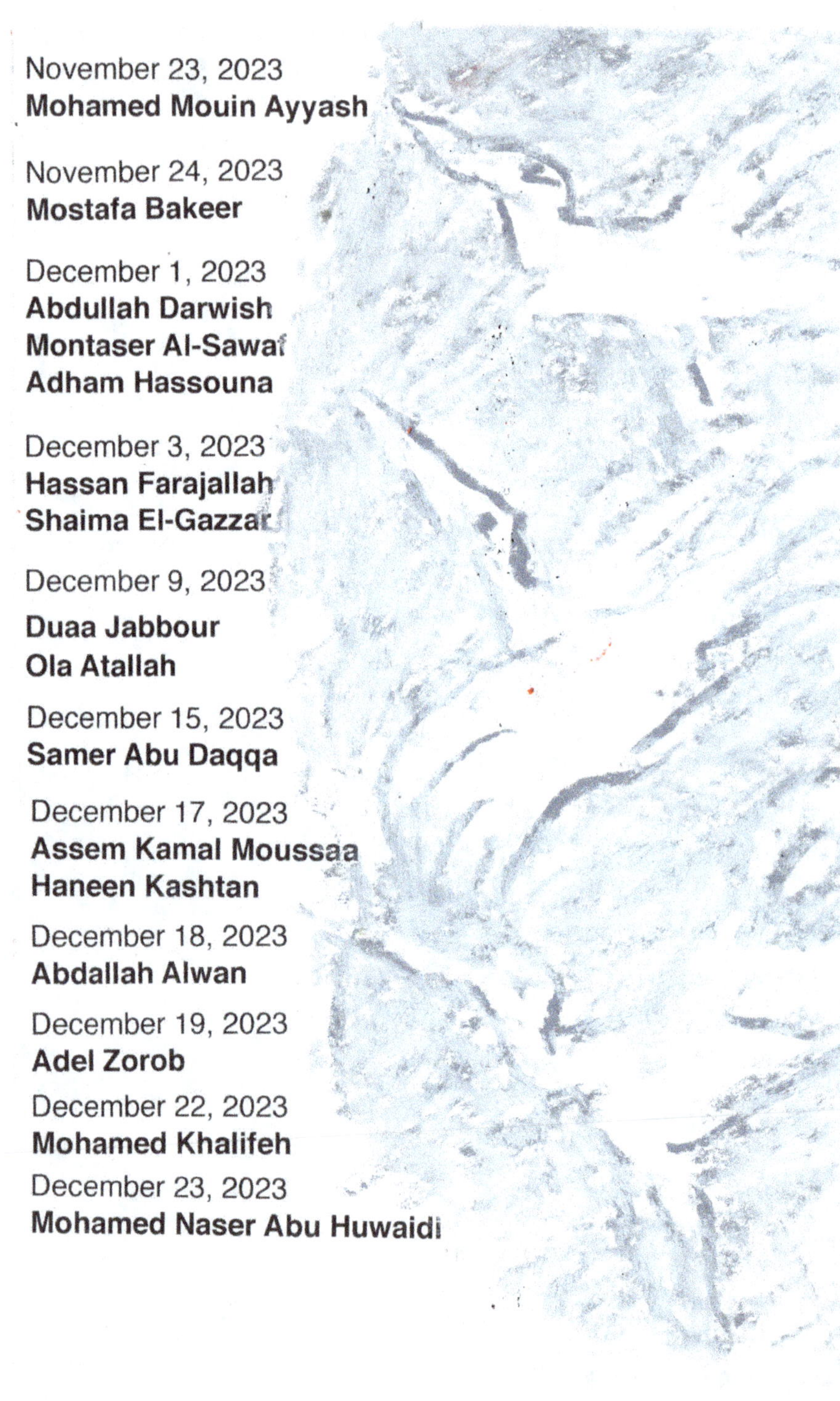

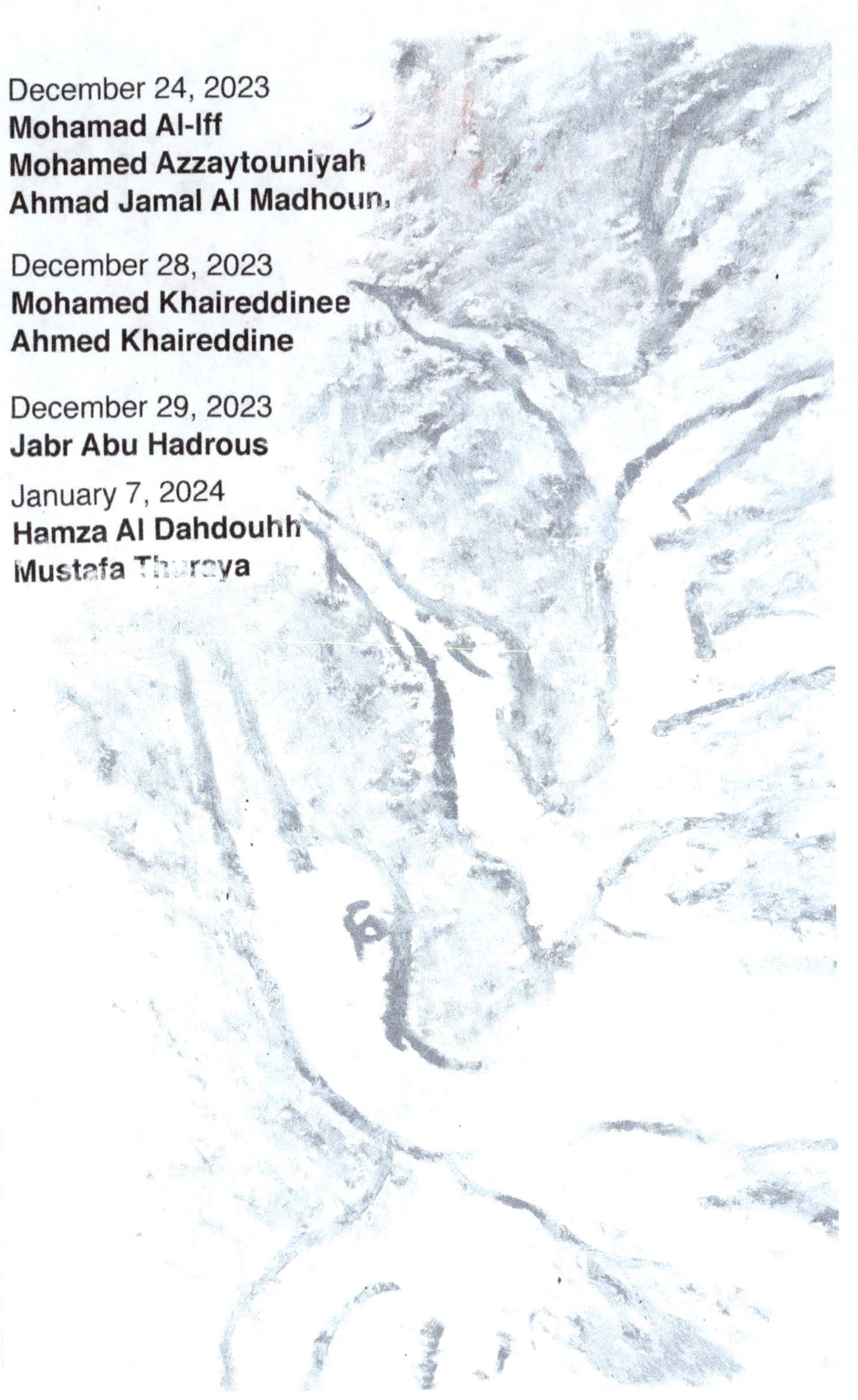

December 24, 2023
Mohamad Al-Iff
Mohamed Azzaytouniyah
Ahmad Jamal Al Madhoun

December 28, 2023
Mohamed Khaireddinee
Ahmed Khaireddine

December 29, 2023
Jabr Abu Hadrous

January 7, 2024
Hamza Al Dahdouhh
Mustafa Thuraya

YOU WHO ARE NOW MEMORY

+ ENCOURAGEMENT TO COMMIT TO THE TRUTH WHICH WE ALL SEEK + NEED

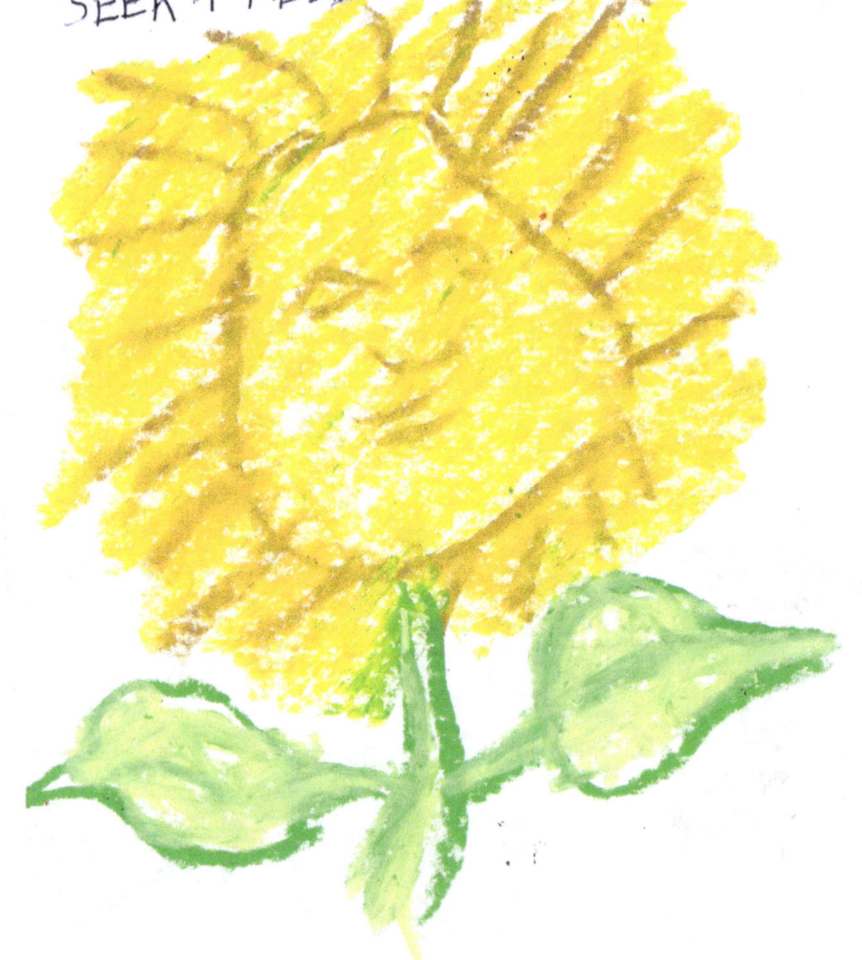

POSSIBILITARIAN

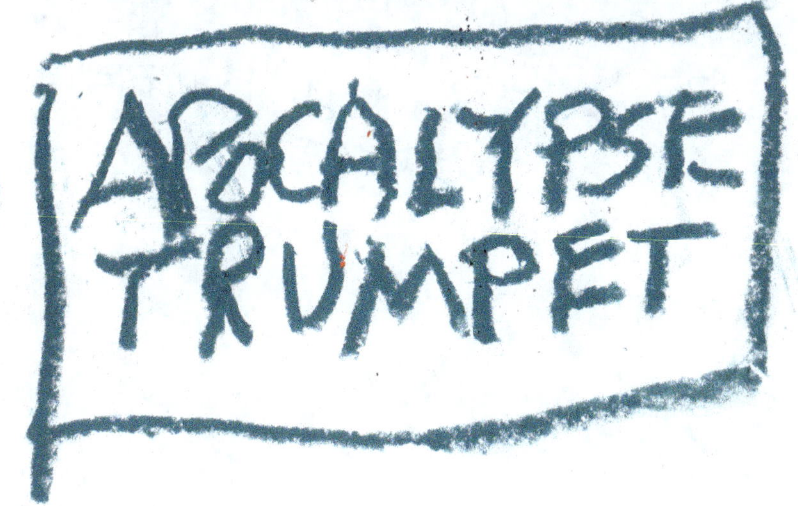

TODAY HOW MANY

BABIES TODDLERS KIDS MOMS
GRANDMAS GRANDPAS DADS
SISTERS BROTHERS AUNTS UNCLES
SLATED FOR DEATH BY WHOM
BY WHAT AUTHORITY WHAT SONS
WHAT FACES WHAT DAUGHTERS
WHAT HANDS WHAT INDUSTRY
WHOSE EYES

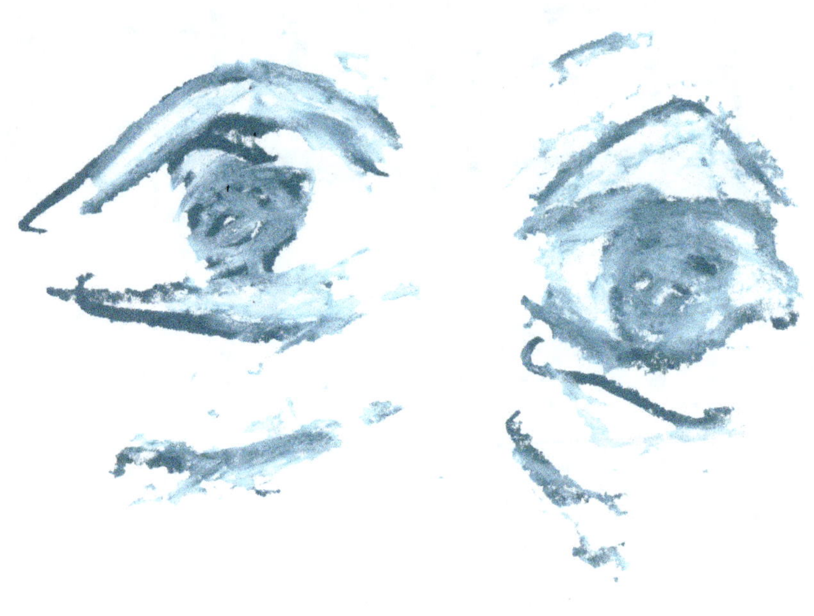

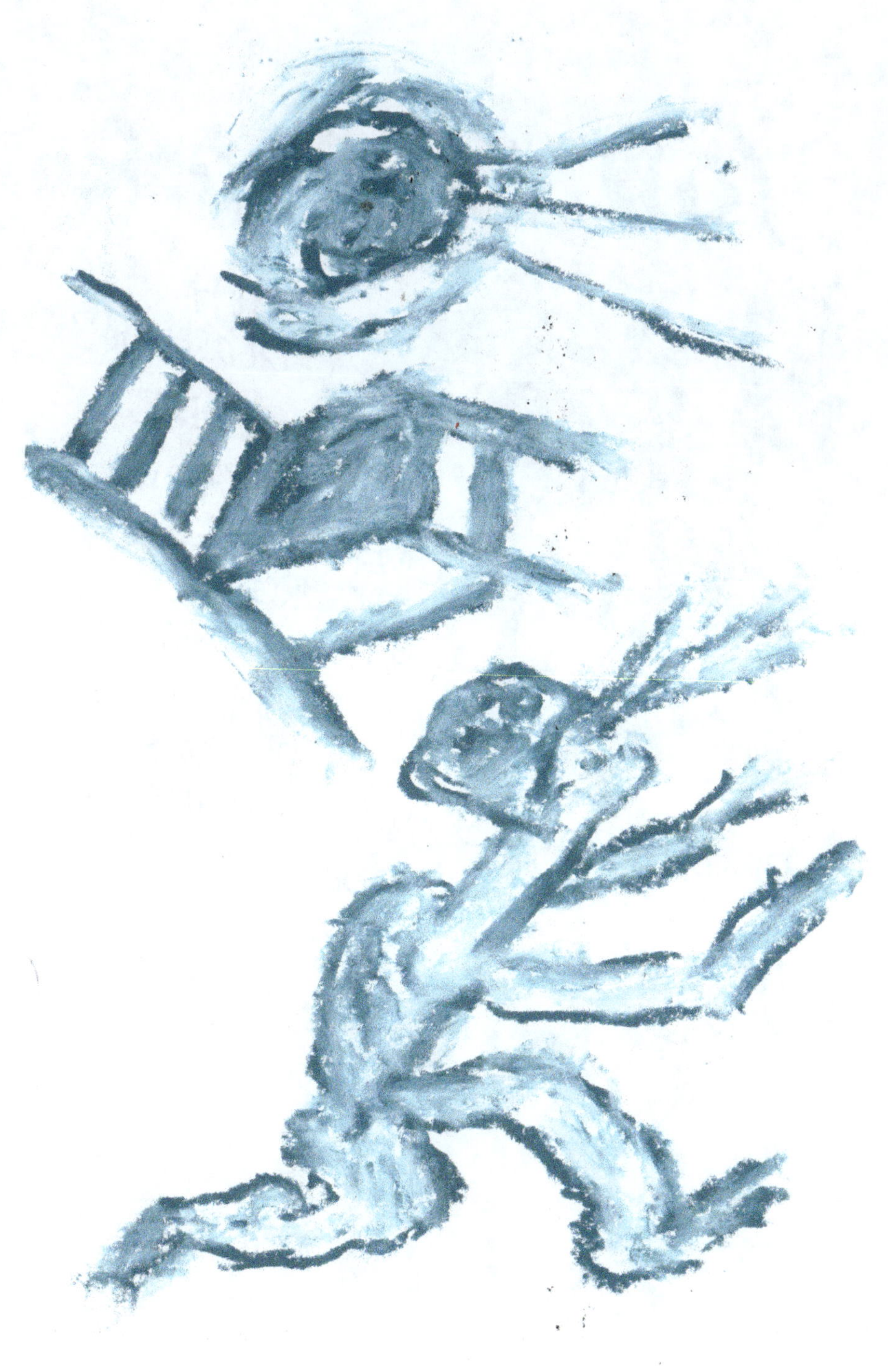

YOU BROTHER

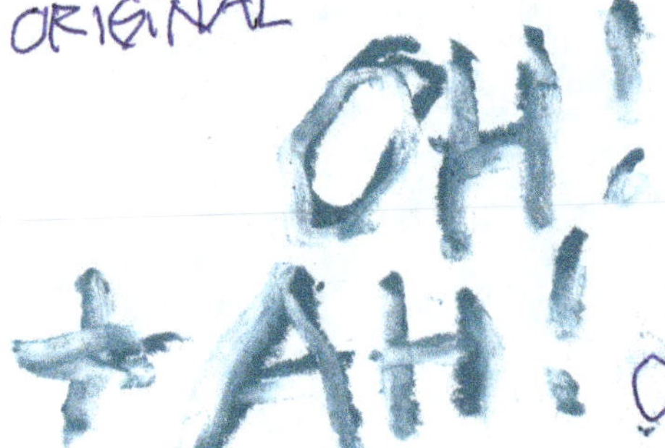

WHICH
BROTHER?
BROTHER
ANONYMOUS
OVERWORKED
WORKFORCELER
WHO CAN'T RETURN
HOME WITHOUT THE
USUAL POSTWORK
DISCOMFORT IN STOMACH + VEINS
WITHOUT SWALLOWING OR CHEWING
THE WORK'S SENSE, SHOUTING THE
ORIGINAL

OH!
+ AH!   OF EXISTENCE

WHILE UNDER ATTACK
FROM SUGARY EVIL + CERTIFIED LIES
OF THE SINISTER CLOWNS WHO NEED
HIS VOTES

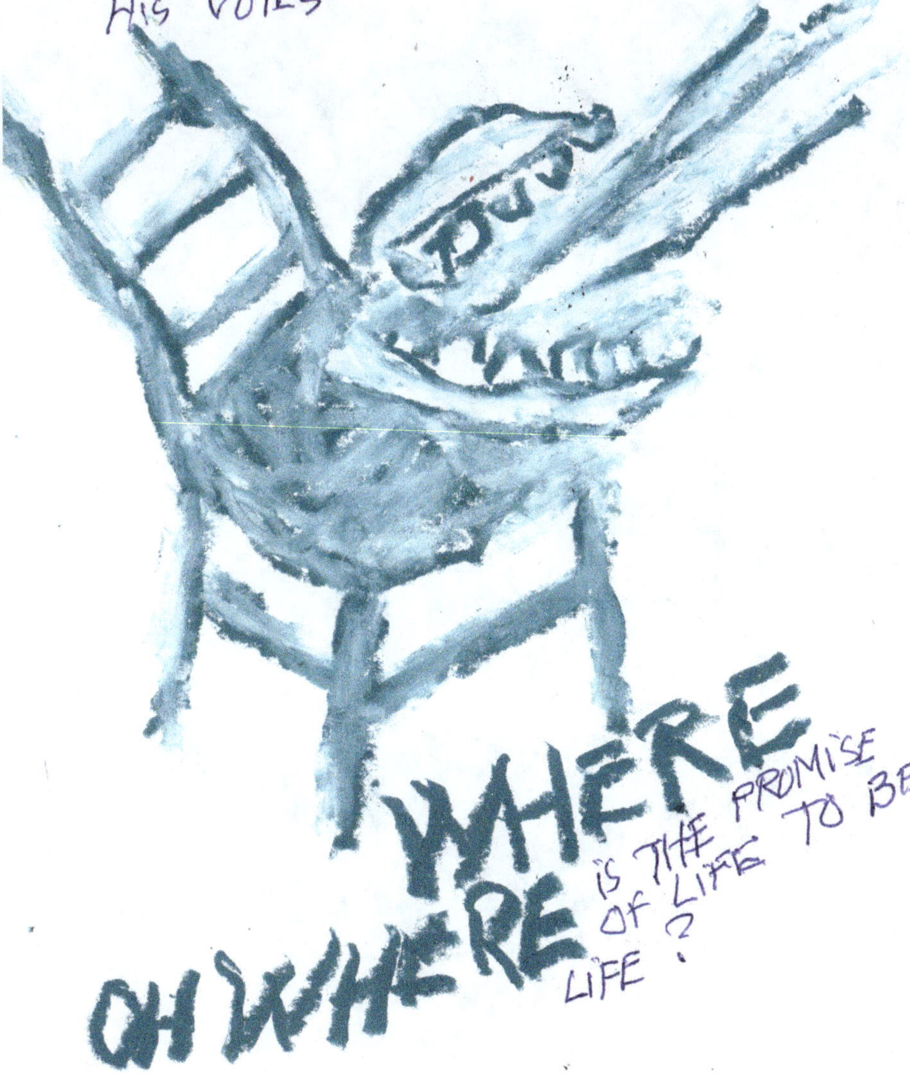

WHERE
OH WHERE
IS THE PROMISE
OF LIFE TO BE
LIFE ?

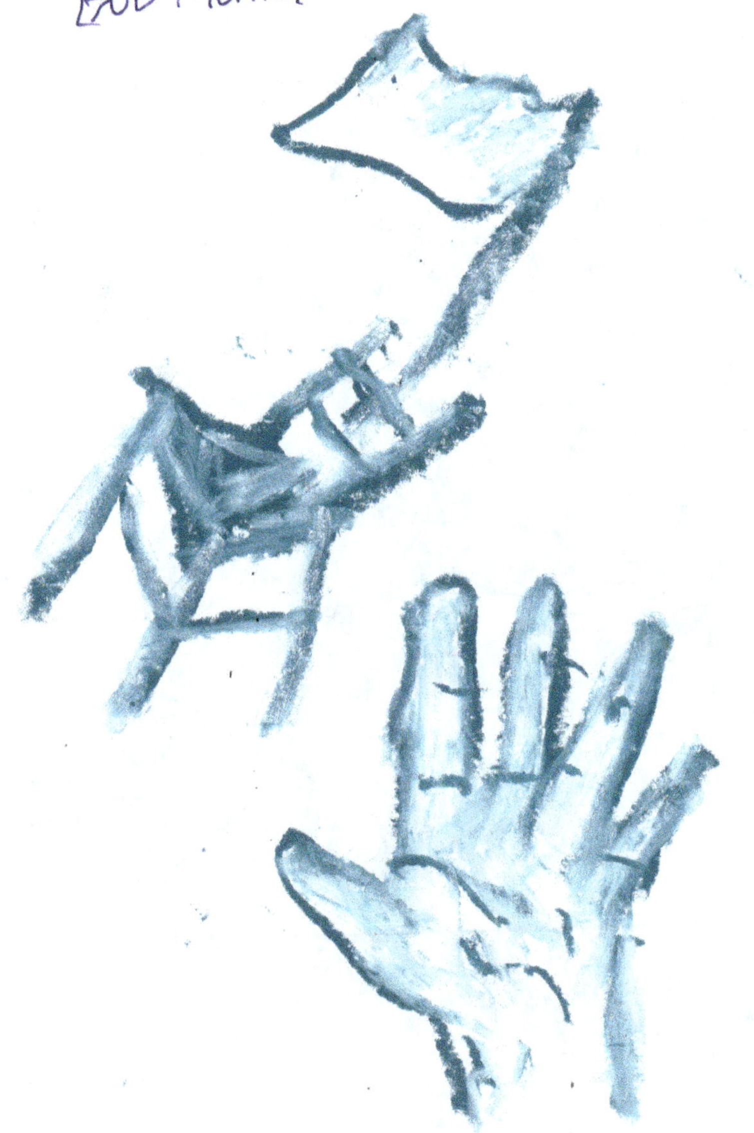

ONLY THE DISGUSTING
AUTHORITY ECONOMY + ITS DISGUSTING
GOD MONEY

WHERE IS THE GLORIOUS UNPREDICTABILITY OF LIFE'S SNOWFLAKES FLOCKING OVER OUR MOTHER DIRT'S BELLY? WHERE IS OUR FIERCE + FURIOUS, GOING ASTRAY FIRST TO THE EVERYWHERE (NOT A CHANCE!) THEN TO THE NOWHERE (ALSO NEGATIVE!) THEN BACK TO THE MINIATURE VACATION FROM WORK — CALLED HOME, THE OBLIGATORY ESSENTIALISM WHICH JUSTIFIES THE ABSENCE OF LIFE + ITS PROMISED GLORY

WHERE?

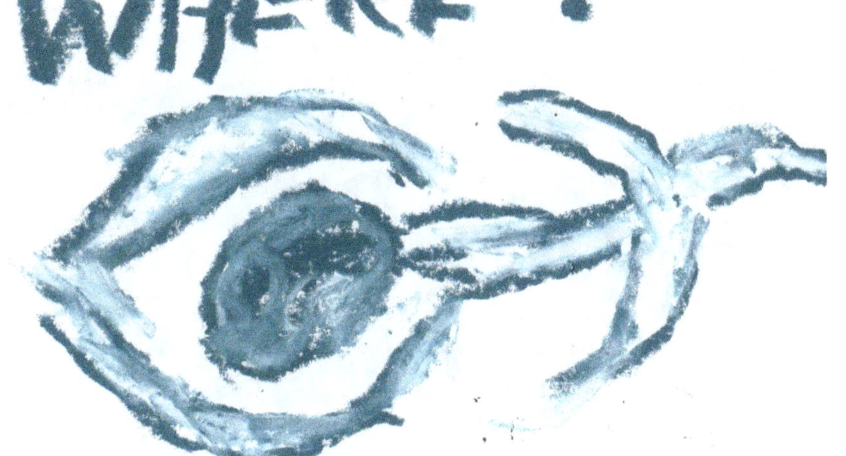

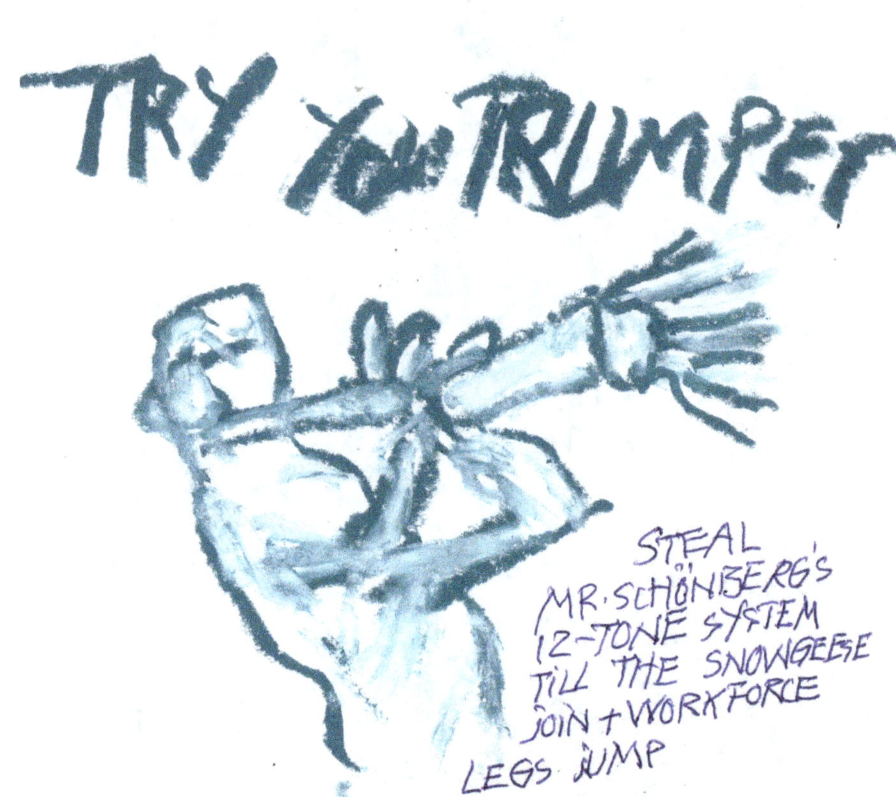

TRY You TRUMPET
STEAL
MR. SCHÖNBERG'S
12-TONE SYSTEM
TILL THE SNOWGEESE
JOIN + WORKFORCE
LEGS JUMP
+ALL DUTIFUL DEGENERATE
OBSERVANCES OF DECREPIT LIFE
DROP DEAD
+GLORY
REIGNS
NEVERTHELESS

POSSIBILITARIAN

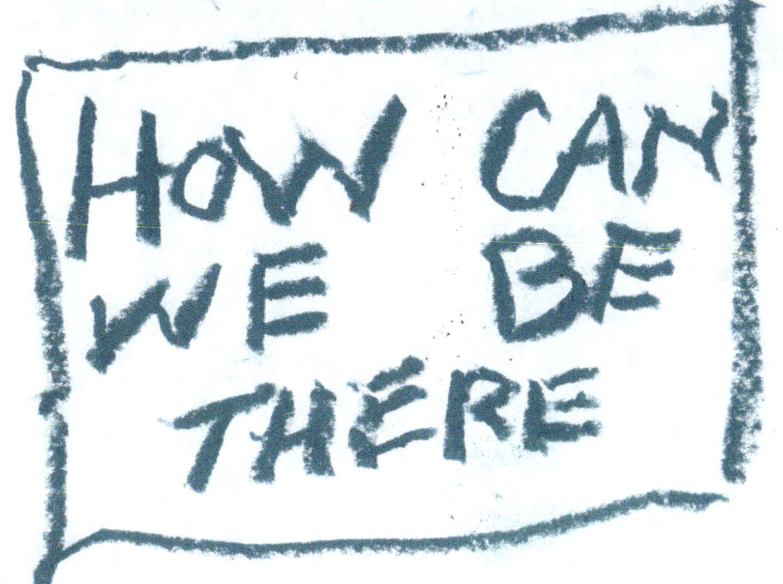

ARE THEY CHILDREN
WHO ARE SNAKES THAT THEY
FEAR?
WHO ARE THEY?

CAN WE AFFORD

TO BE CHILDREN + FAIL THEM
AS THEY ARE KILLED?

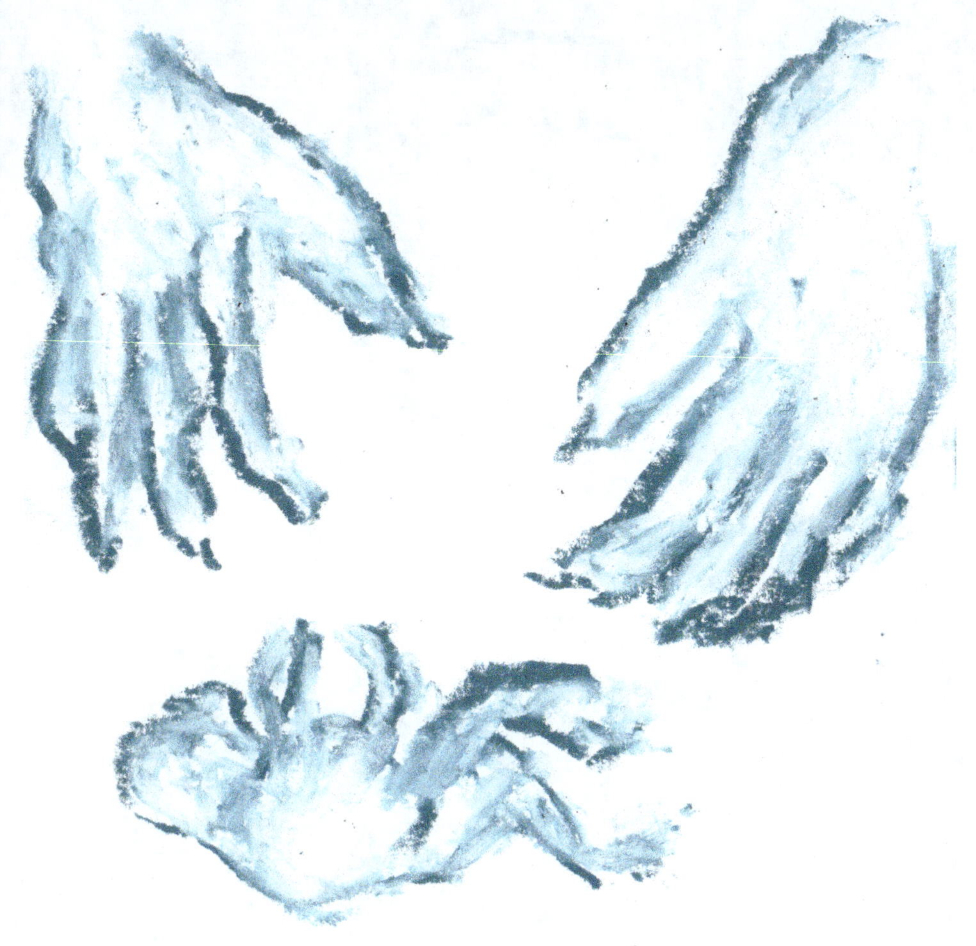

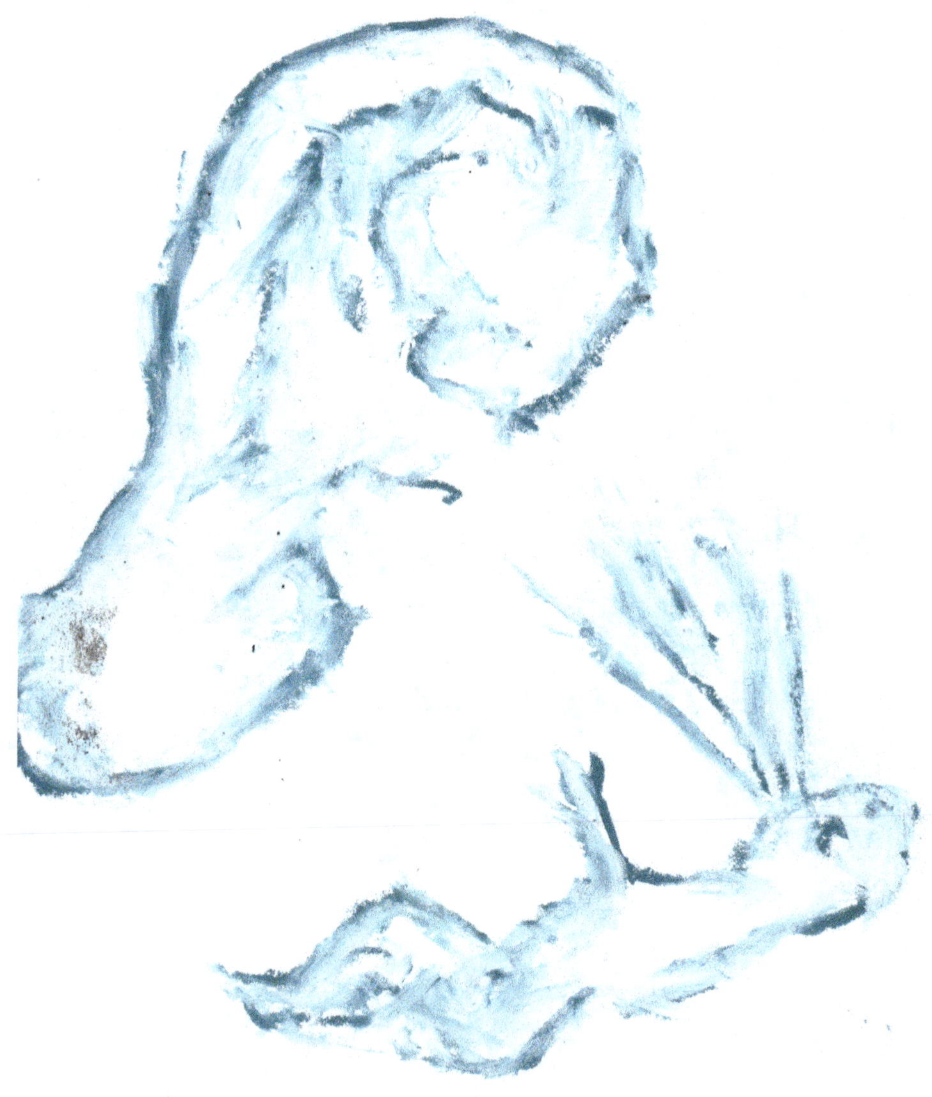

ARE OUR EARS
THERE WHEN THEY
SCREAM?

CAN WE AFFORD TO NOT BE THERE?

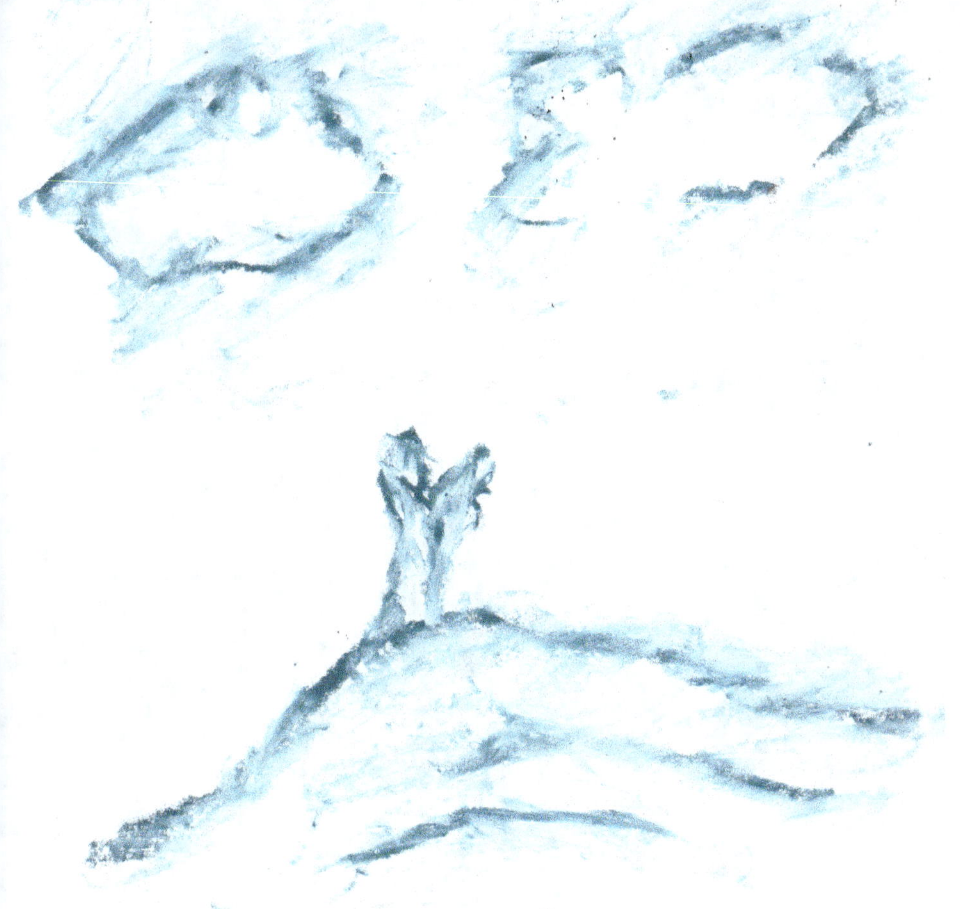

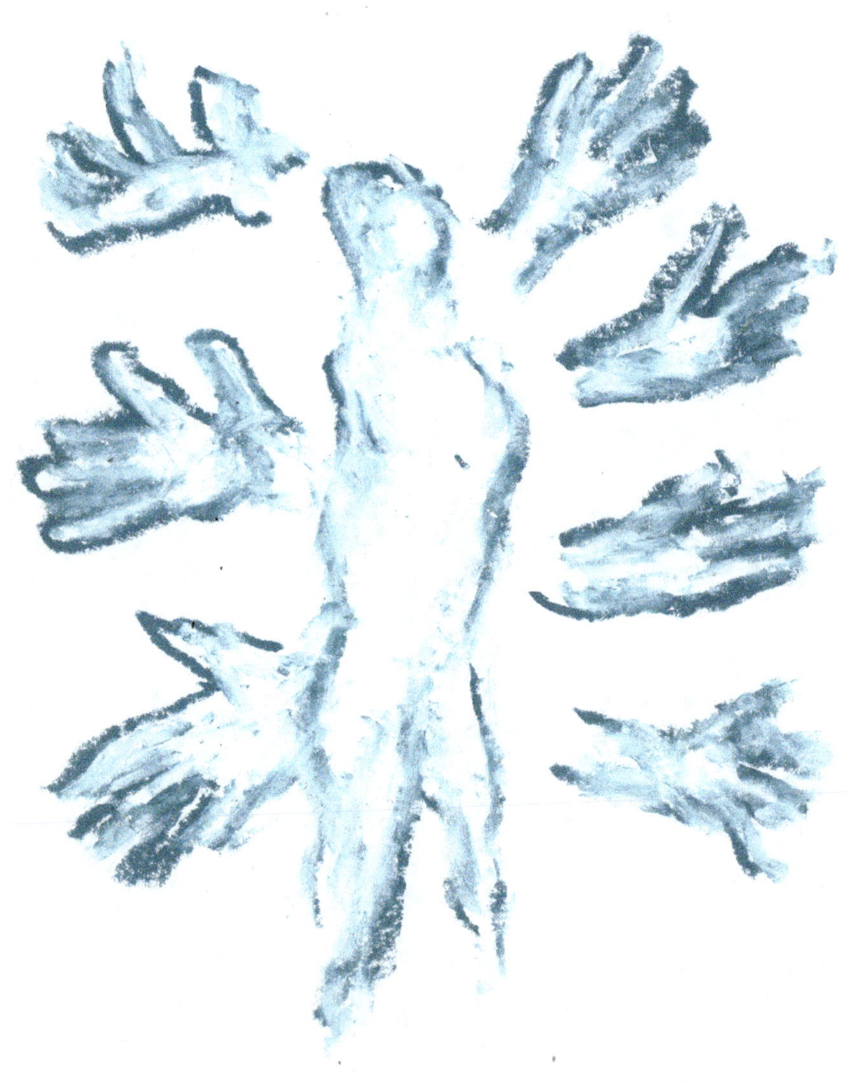

HOW CAN WE
DE + NOT BE THERE?

HOW CAN WE BE THERE?

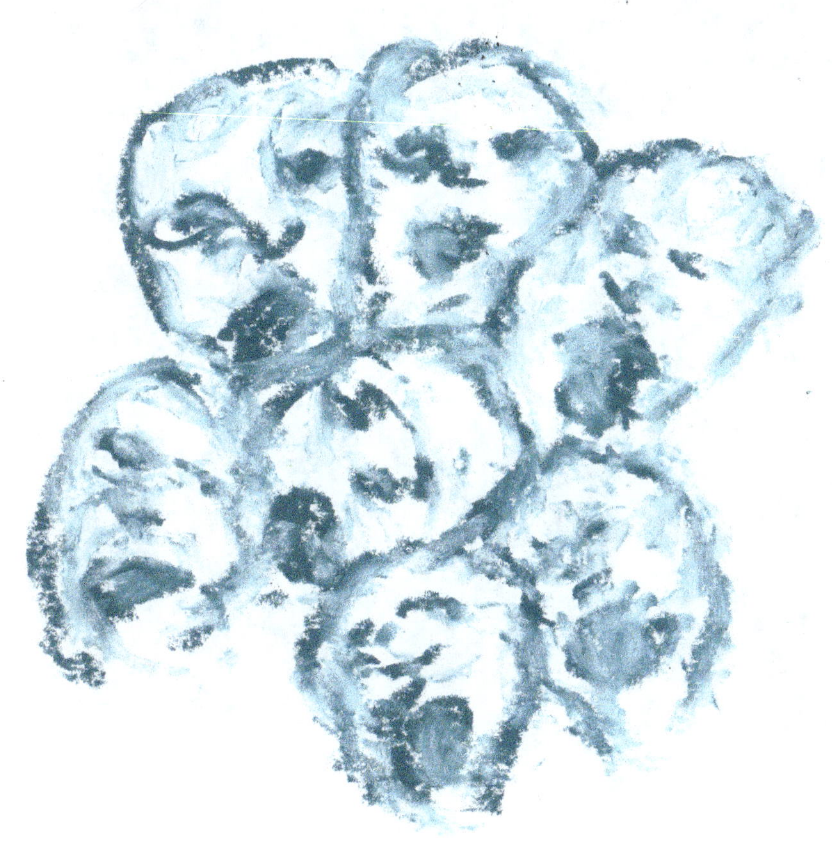

iS THERE SUCH

A THING AS BEING NOT THERE?

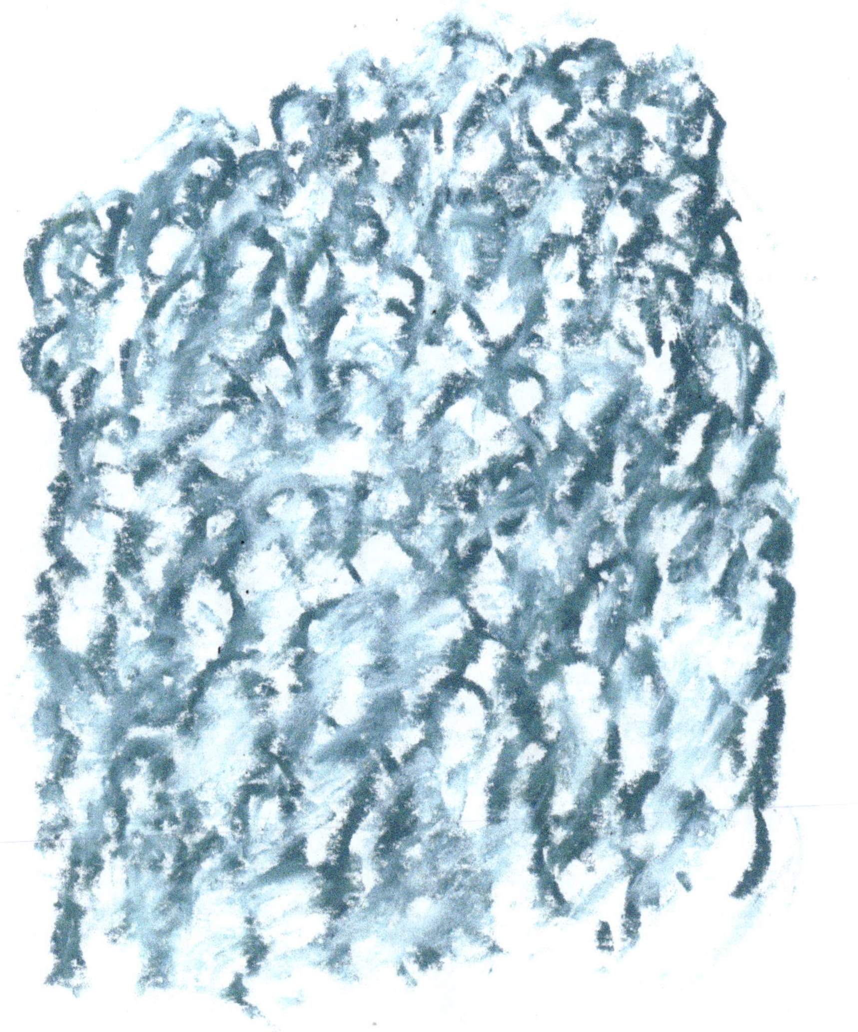

Is Life Life?

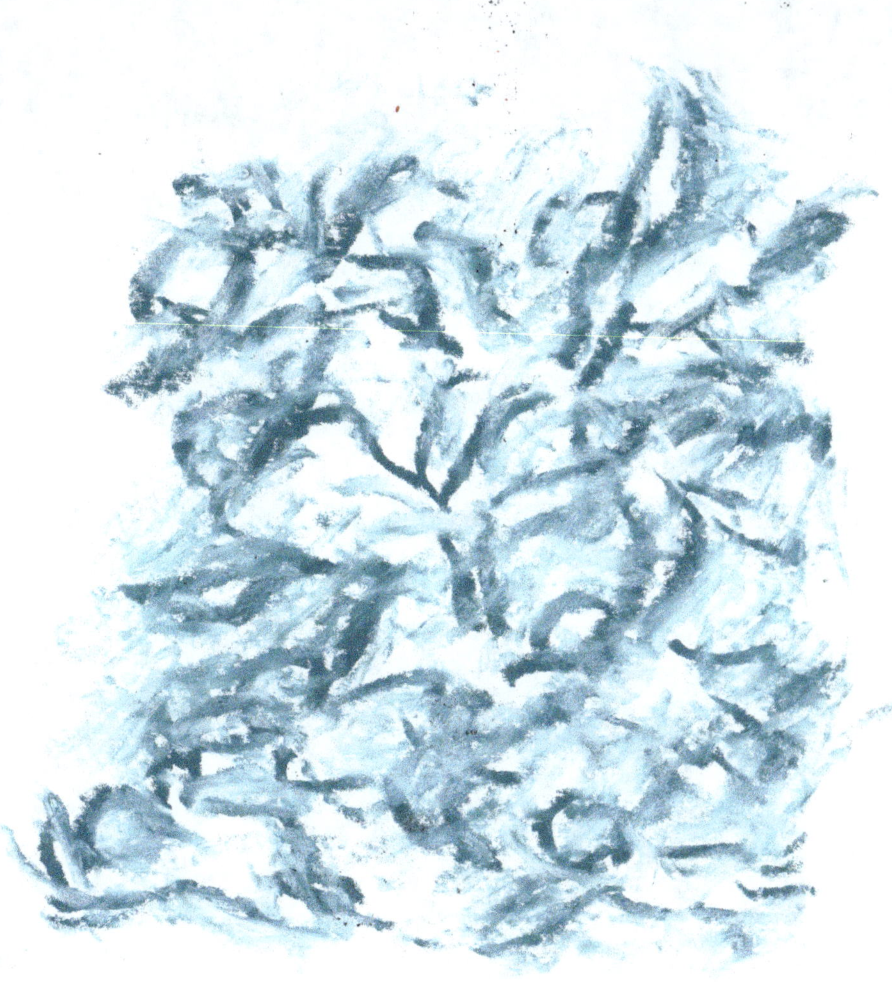

POSSIBILITARIAN

MOTHERS' LOVE

FOR THE MOTHERS WHO ARE BEING MOWED DOWN

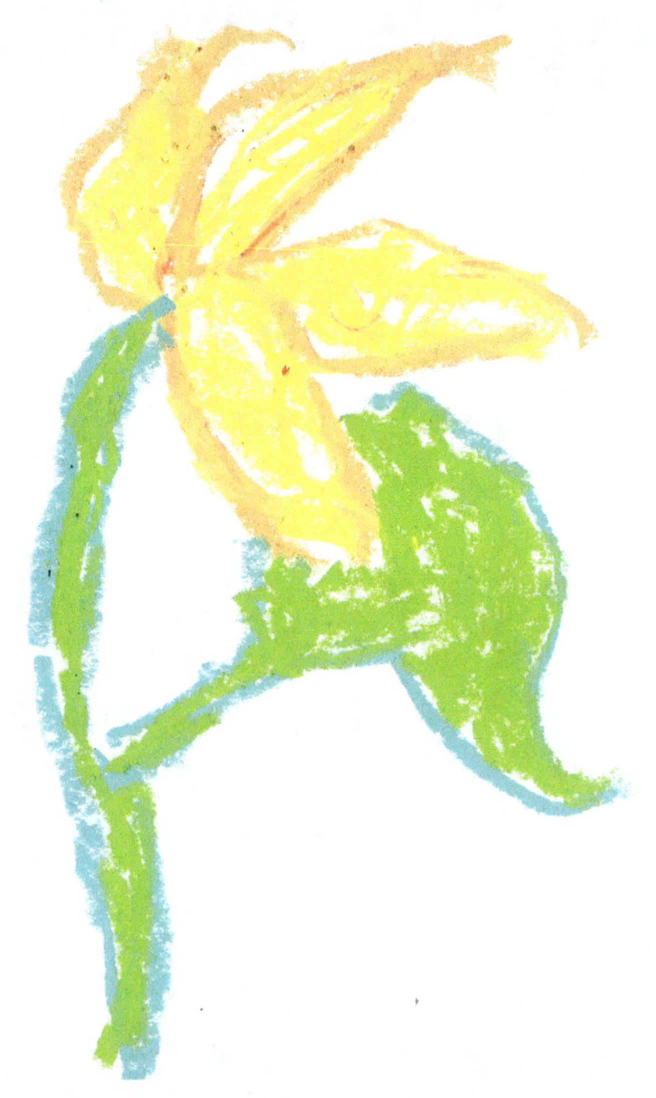

LOVE MEANS

NOT ALONE BUT ACCOMPANIED
BY LOVE

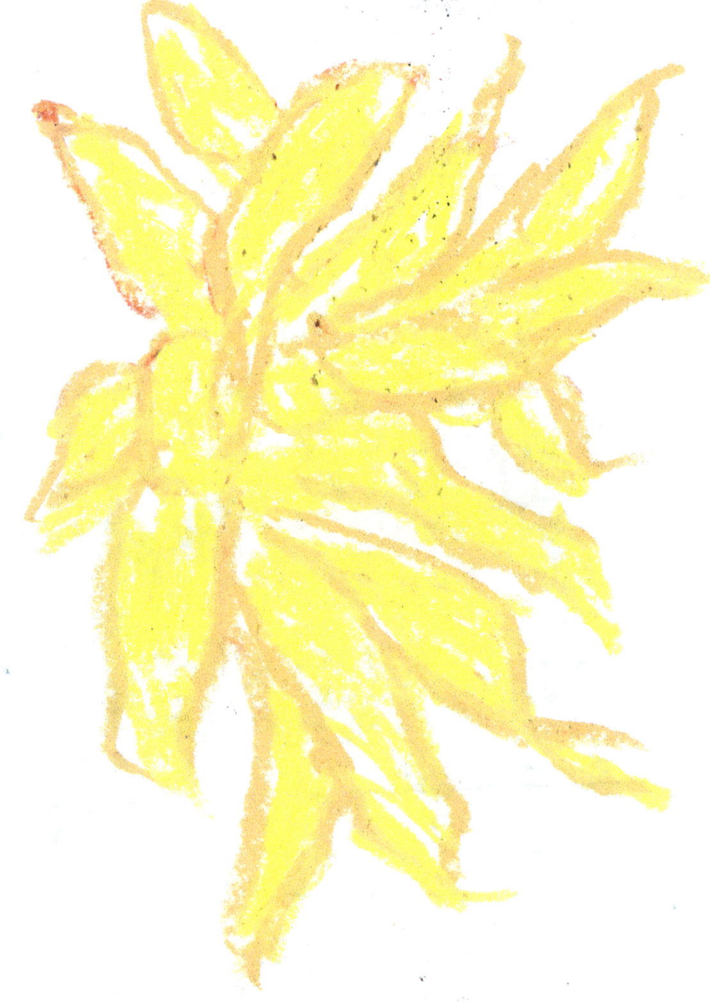

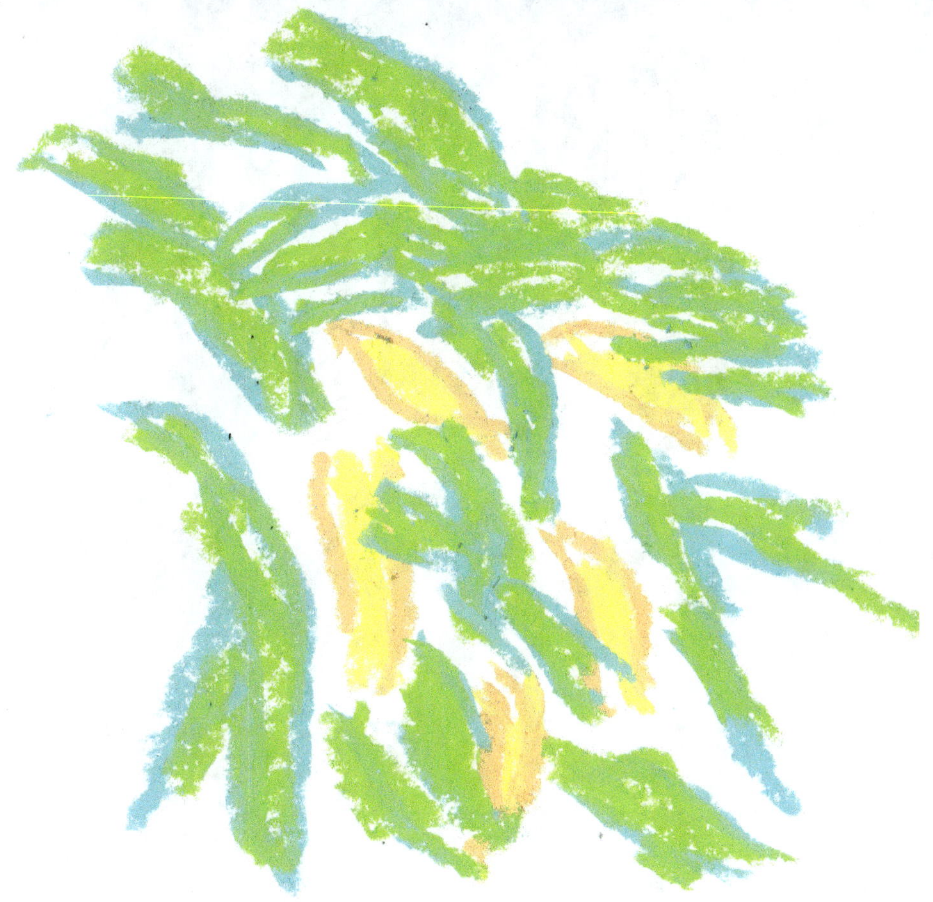

LOVE MOWED DOWN BY THE HUNDREDS DOES NOT ACCOMPANY BUT IS LEFT ALONE

THE ALONE

is made by the facilitators

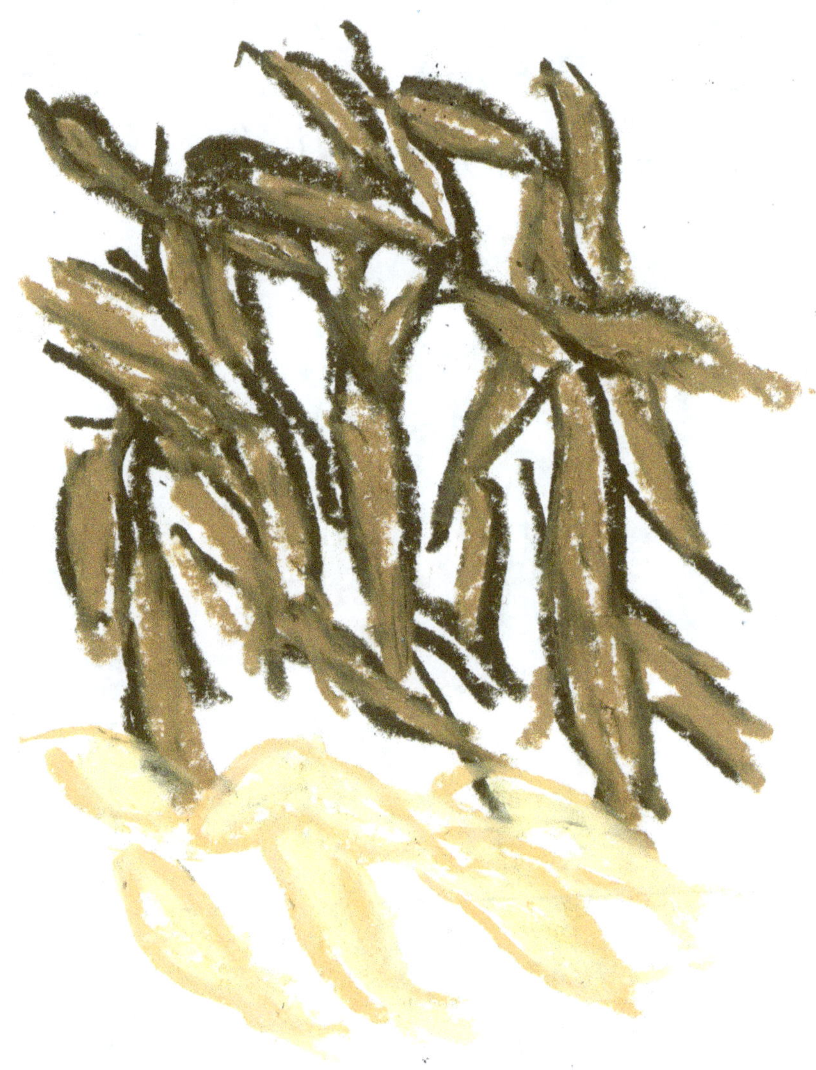

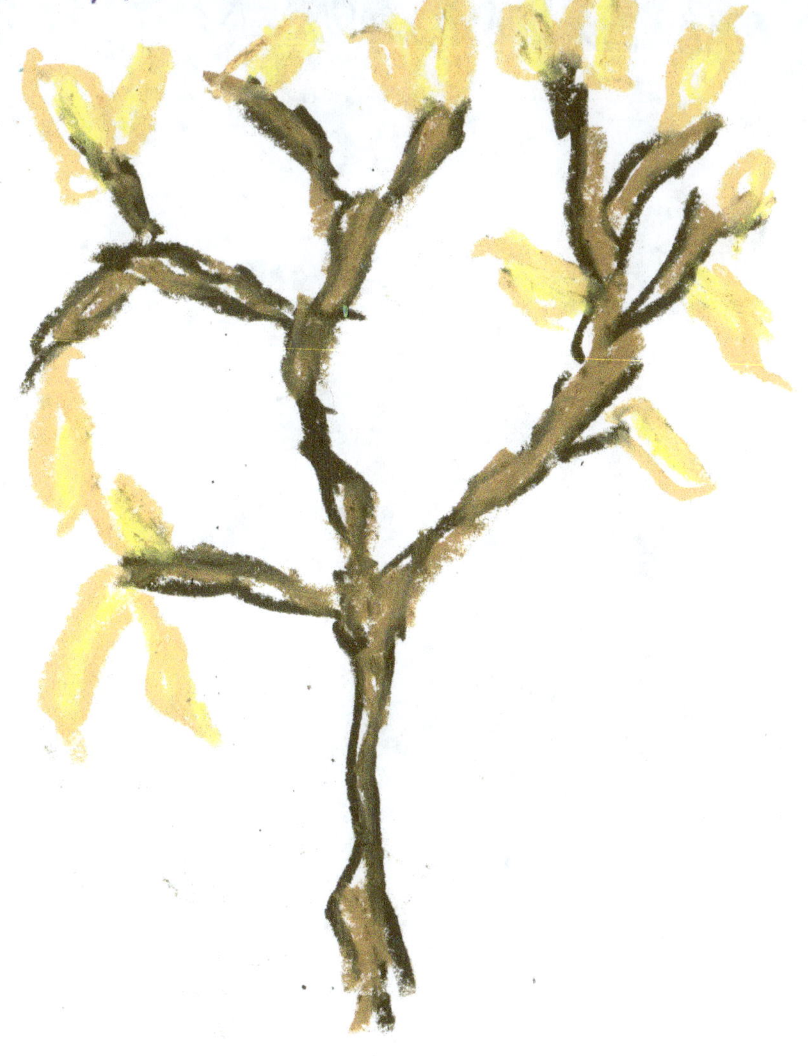

WE MUST BE
MOTHERS BECAUSE OF THE
MOWED DOWN MOTHERS

ASSIGNED

TO MOTHERHOOD BY THE MOWED DOWN MOTHERS

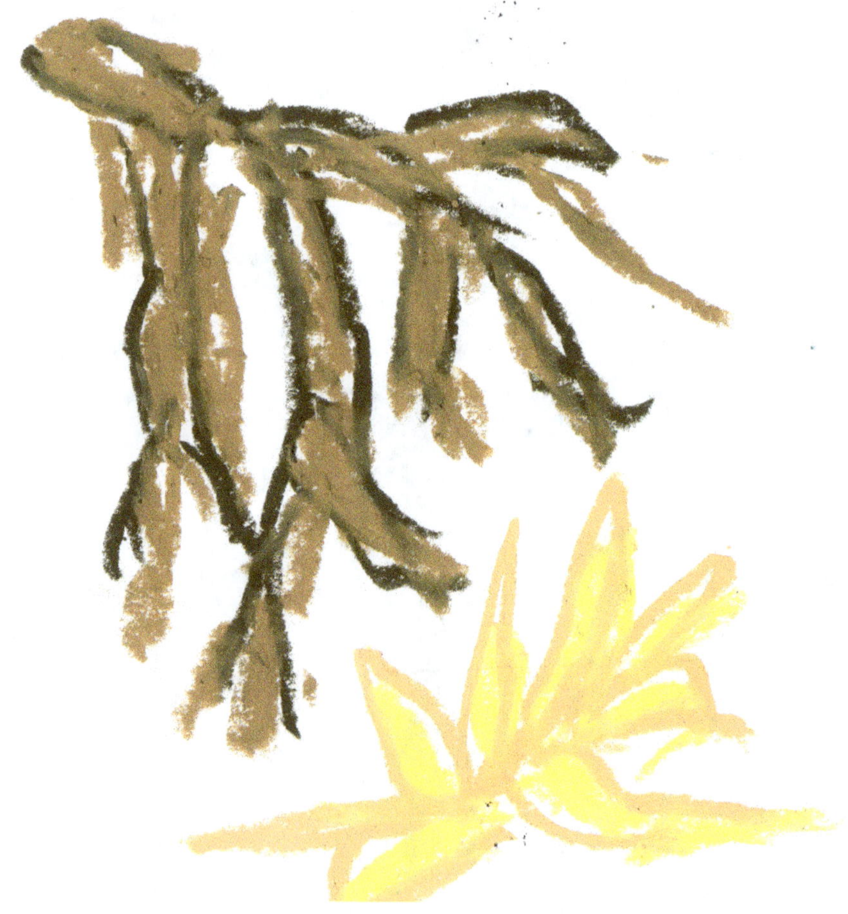

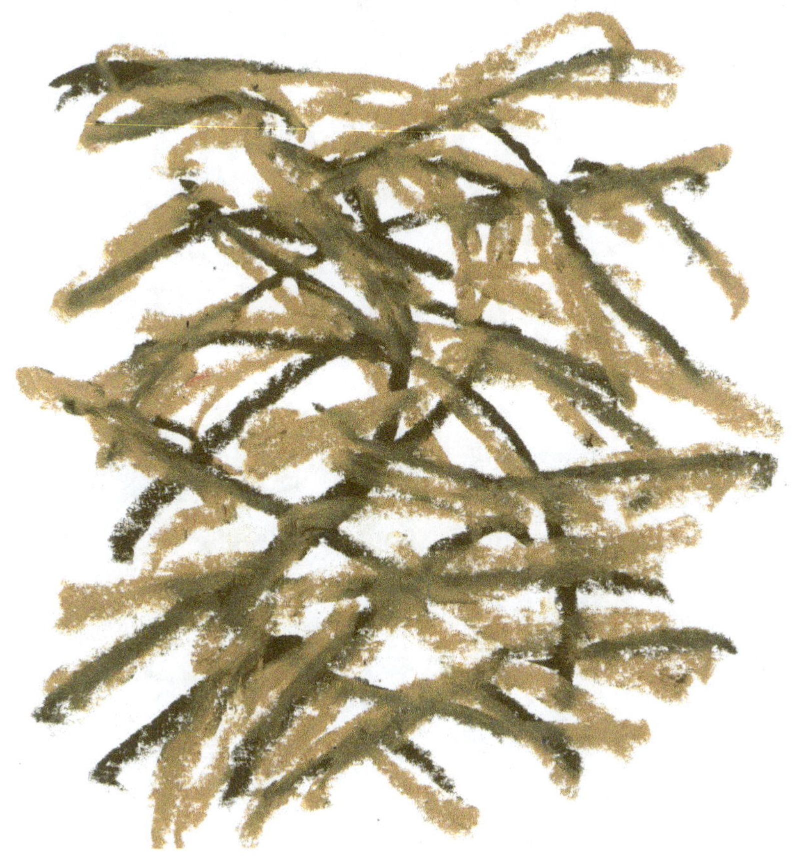

WE WILL
FIGHT BITE SMITE
TIL THE FACILITATORS
ARE FACILITATED

FOR LOVE

THE ACCOMPANIST

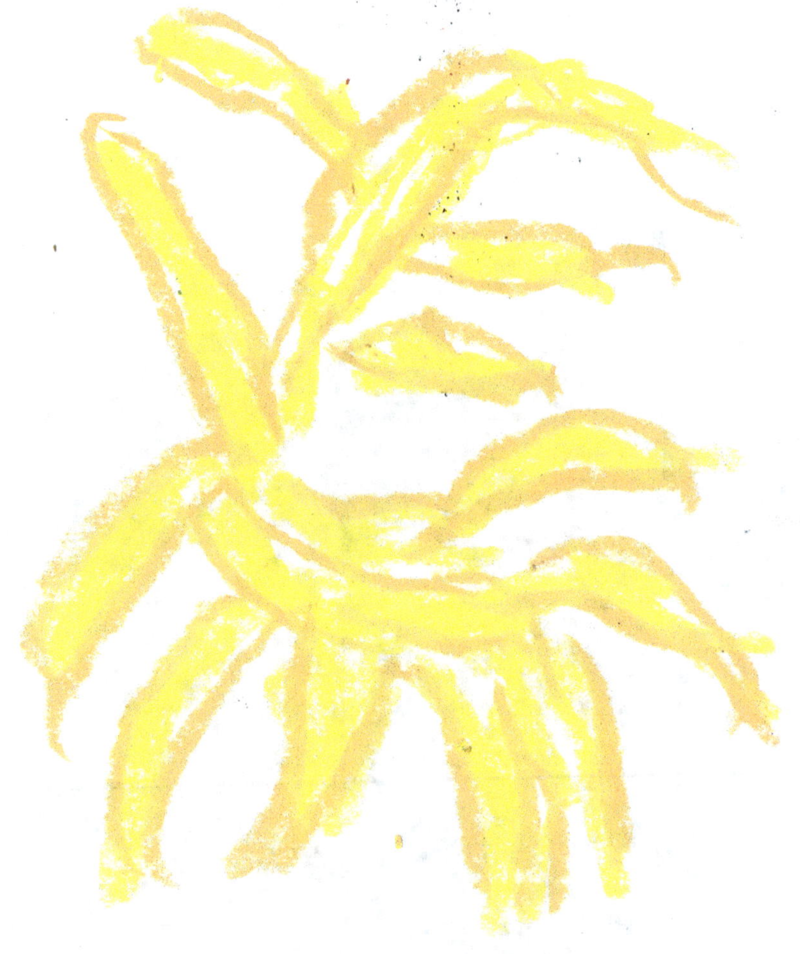

POSSIBITARIAN

RISE

WE THE MONKED DOWN MOTHERS OF HEAVEN MADE INTO HELL BY HELL SPECIALISTS WHO CLAIM LIFE BUT MEAN DEATH

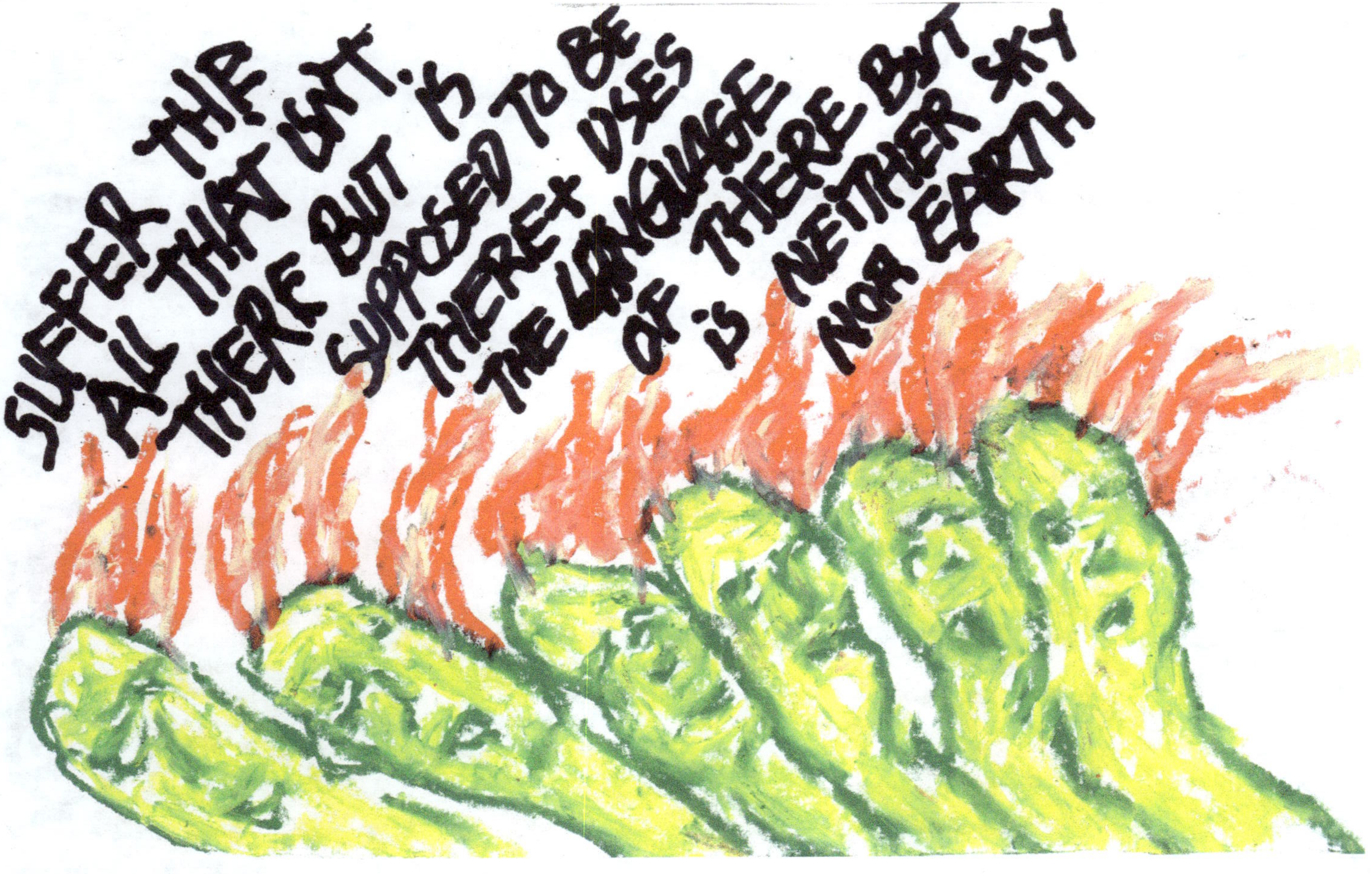

SUFFER THE UNT. IS
ALL THAT ISN'T
THERE BUT IS
SUPPOSED TO BE
THERE+ USES
THE LANGUAGE
OF THERE BUT
IS NEITHER SKY
NOR EARTH

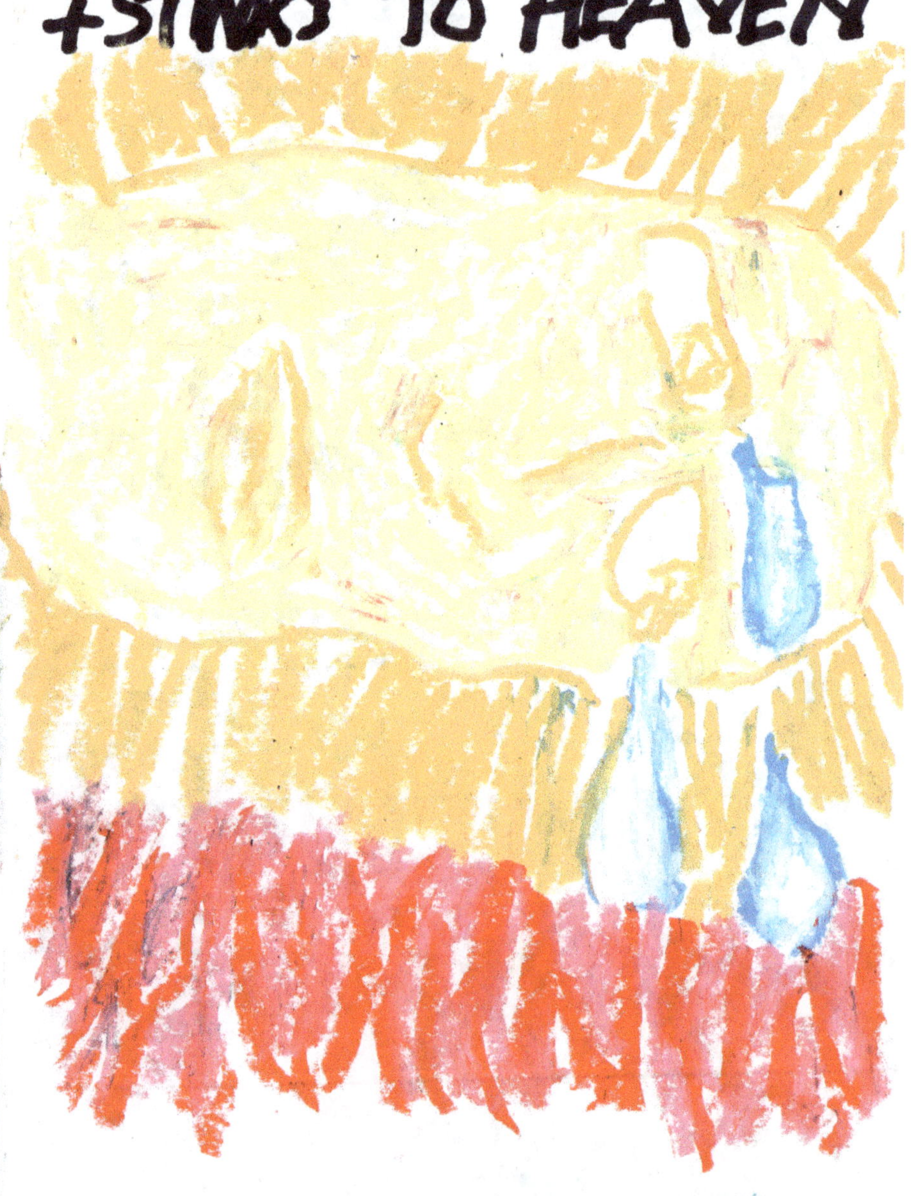

+STINKS TO HEAVEN
FROM THE WOUNDS
IT INFLICTS

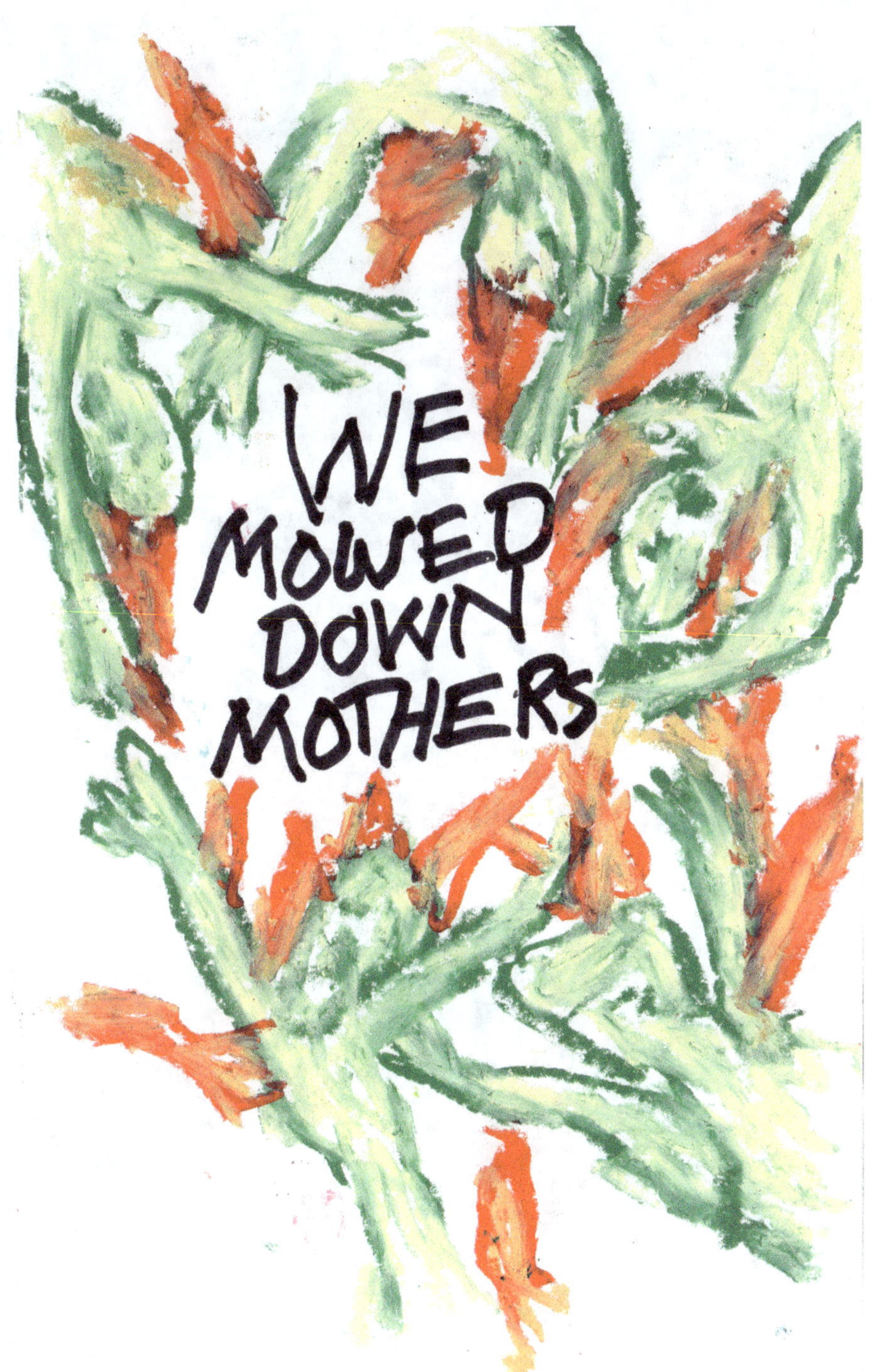

WE
MOWED
DOWN
MOTHERS

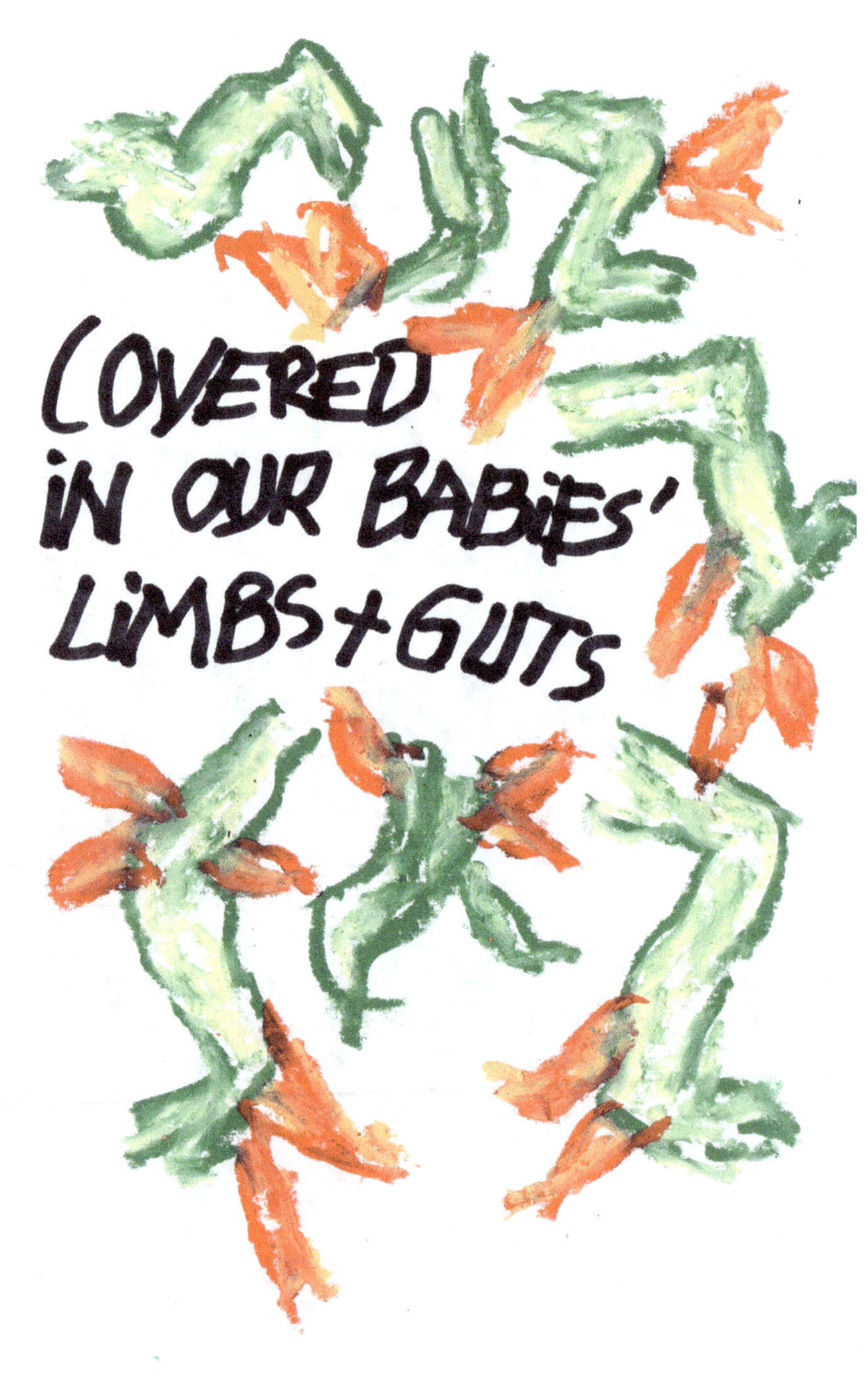

(OVERED
IN OUR BABIES'
LIMBS + GUTS

MADE FOR
DANCE + DIGESTION
BUT SLATED FOR
PAIN

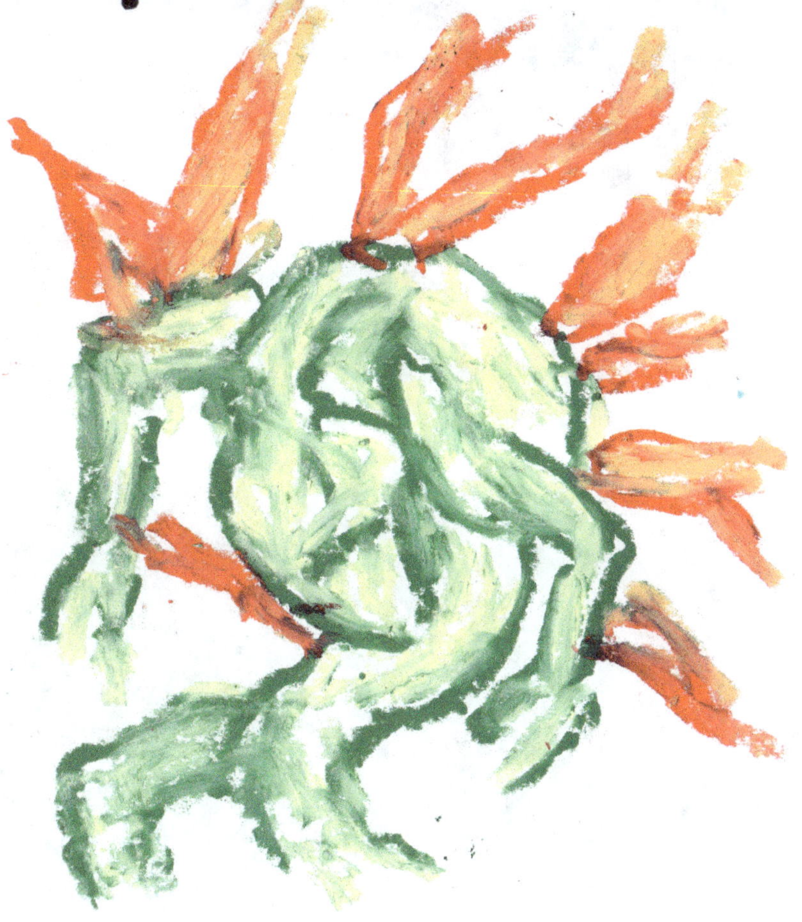

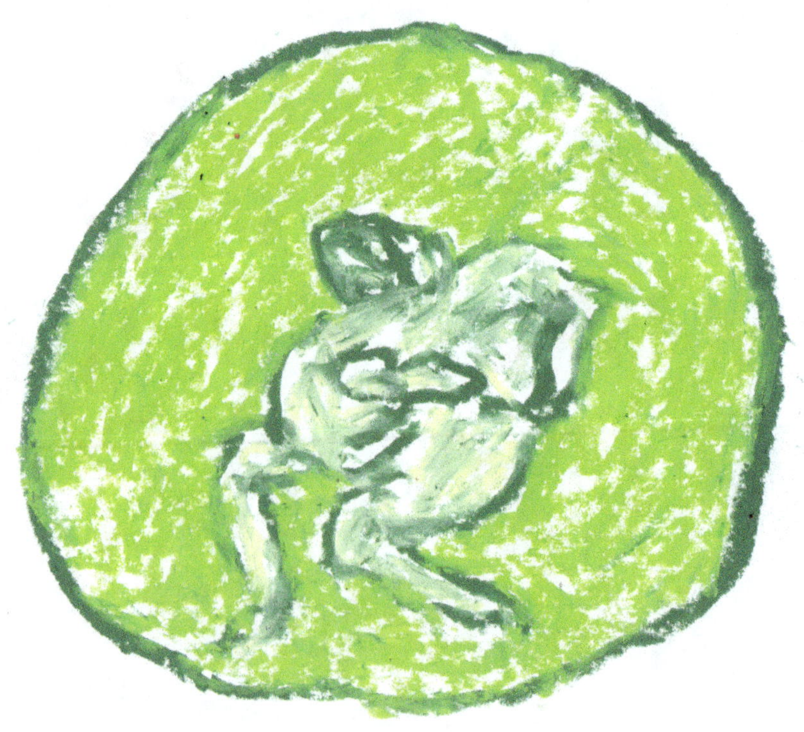
WE THE
MOWED DOWN
MOTHERS OF
THE ALL
DEPRIVED OF
THE ALL

WILL BE THE OPPOSITE
OF THIS DEPRIVED ALL
+ MINDLESSNESS +
HEARTLESSNESS

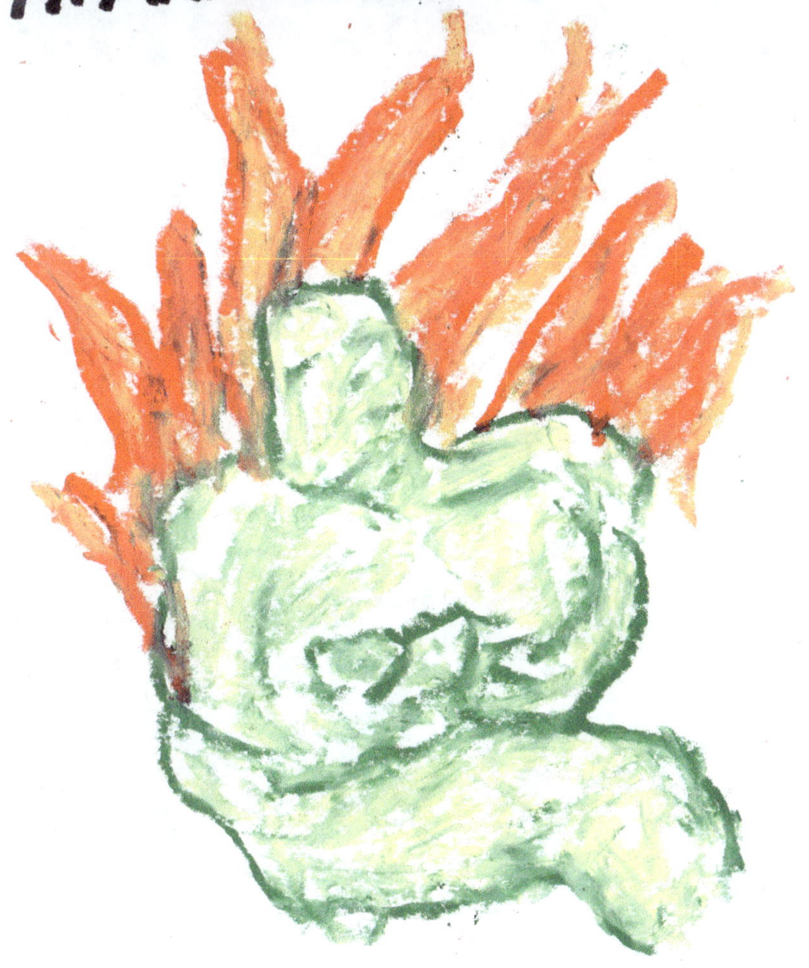

AND RISE
+ RISE

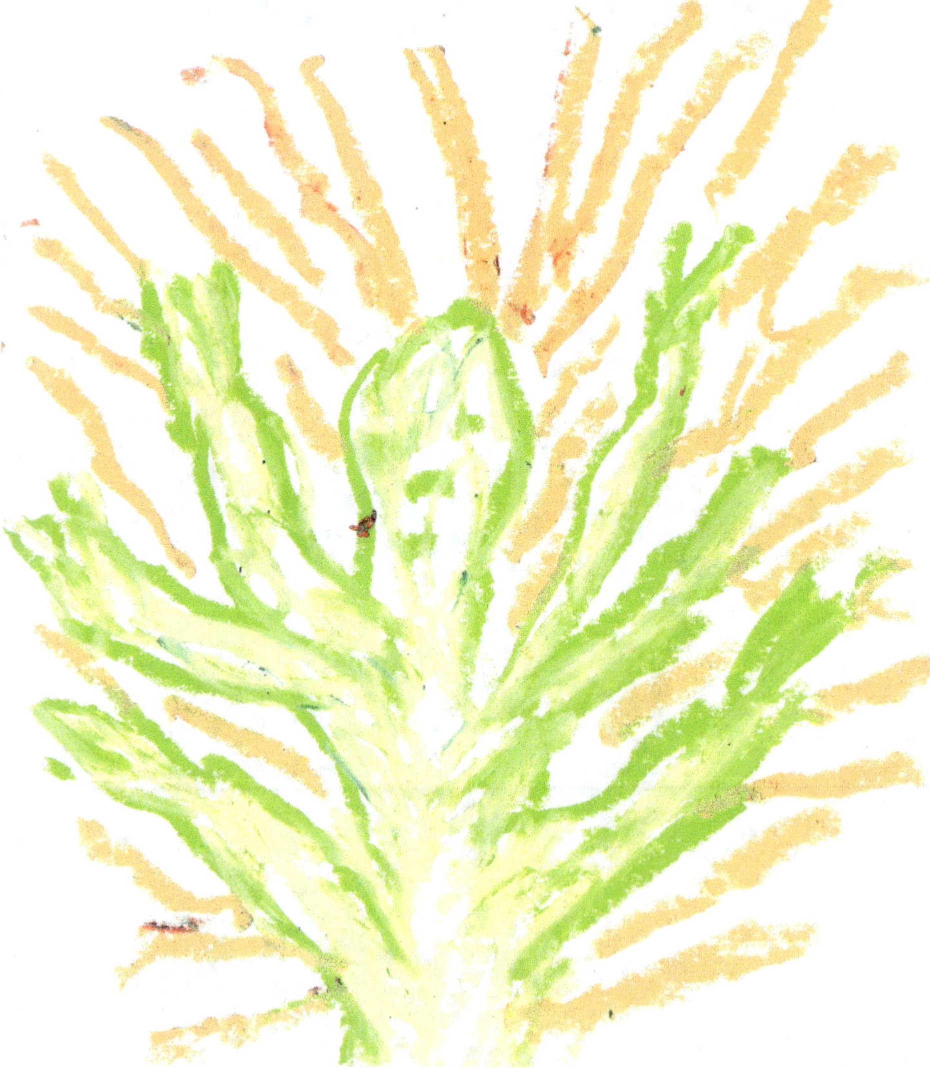

POSSIBILITARIAN

SPIT

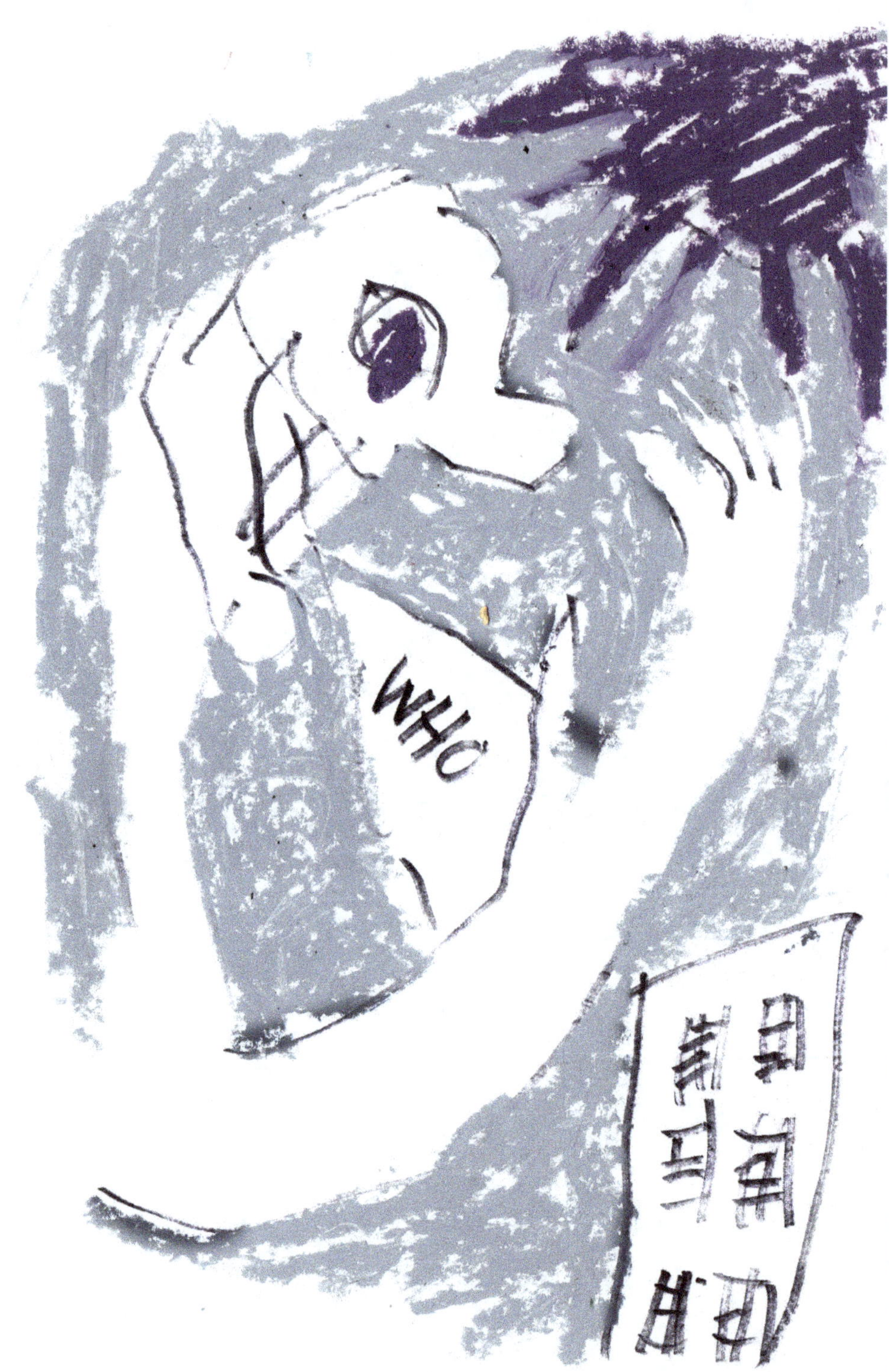

WHO

YOU THE LANGUAGE OF
THE NO-NO-MILLIONS OF FEET
+ MINDS REFUSING THE
SCUM-OF-THE-EARTH IDIOTS
+ HORRORISTS + THEIR WIDELY
ADVERTISED INTENTIONS,
UNAWARE OF THEIR
END-OF-THE-ROAD CAPITALISM
IN ITS DEATH-THROES!
PLEASE DON'T FORGET TO
THROW SHIT AT THEIR SLICK
BLAH-BLAH-VOICES THAT
REFUSE EVEN THE MINIMAL
CEASE-FIRE + TEAR LIMBS
OFF BABIES + DESPAIR
FAMILIES + THE EVERYTHING
+ THEIR CONCRETE HEARTS
HAVE NO KNOWLEDGE

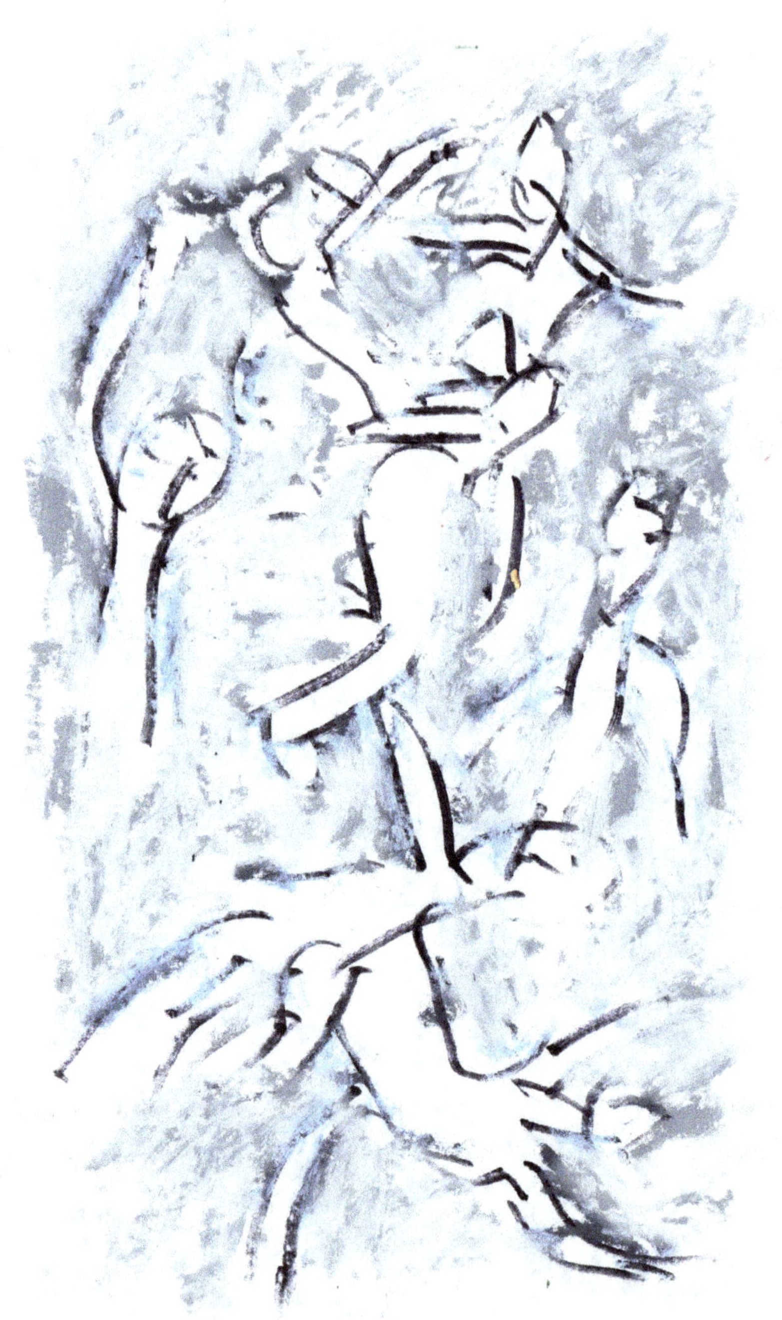

+ OUR SLEEPLESS ASSISTANT
SUFFERING NIGHTS
FAIL THEM ! BY FAILING THIS
HYPOCRACY GOVERNMENT TO
STOP ITS HORROR + PRETEND
TO BE HUMAN FOR 2 MINUTES
+ CALL FOR THE MINIMAL
CEASE-FIRE !
PLEASE DON'T FORGET TO SPIT
INTO THEIR SLICK BLAH-BLAH
FACES!
YES WE MUST COMMIT TO
THAT SHIT : TO NOT LET
THEM GO WHEREEVER THEY
GO, NOT EVEN TO THEIR
ELECTION !

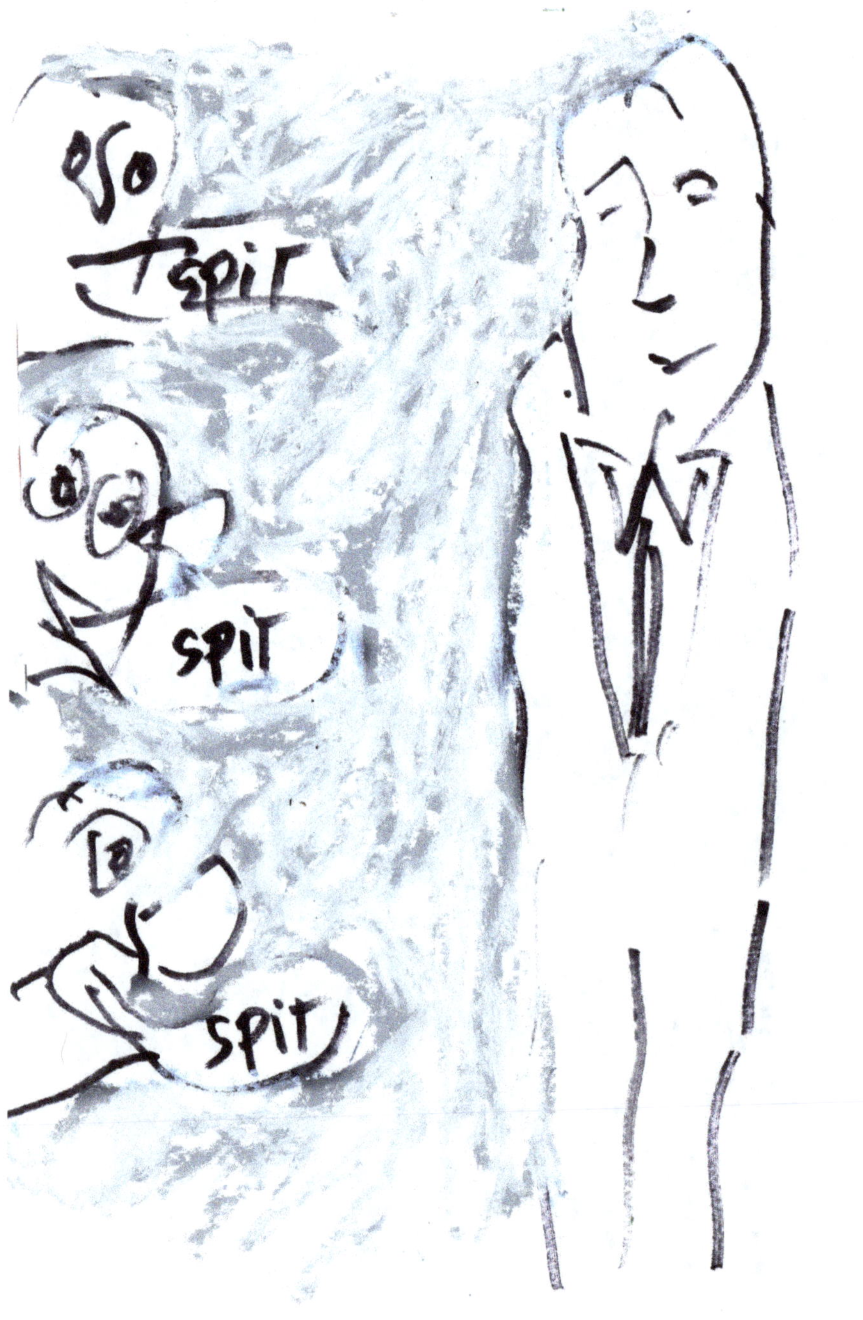
spit
spit
spit

YES OUR SLEEPLESS NIGHTS DEPEND ON THIS! + WE CAN'T BE OR EXIST WITHOUT THIS COMMITMENT TO TOTAL SUFFERING SOLIDARITY WITH THEM WHO ARE MEANT TO BE SLAUGHTER— BEASTS BUT ARE HUMAN BEYOND OUR HUMANITY!

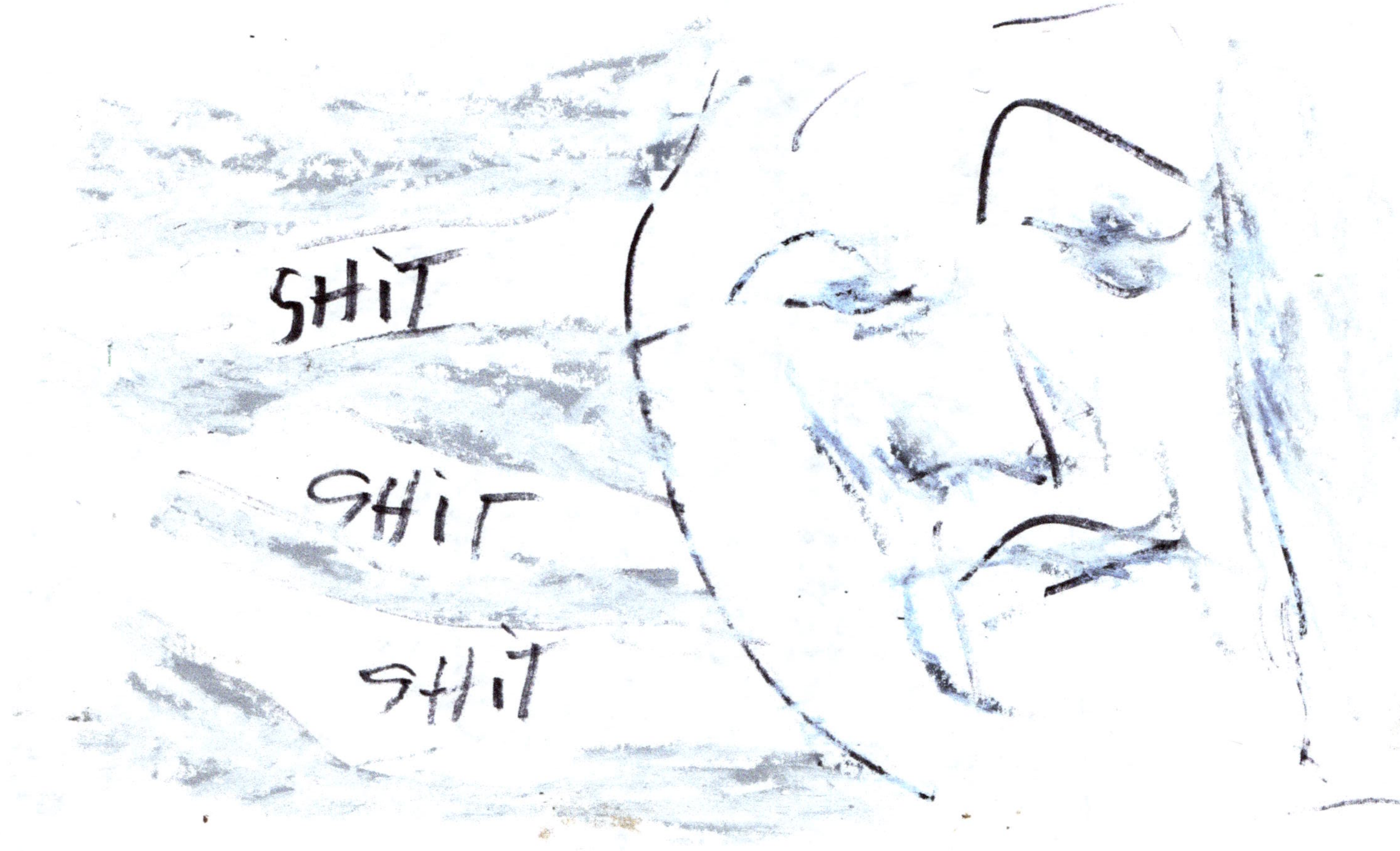

SHiT
SHiT
SHiT

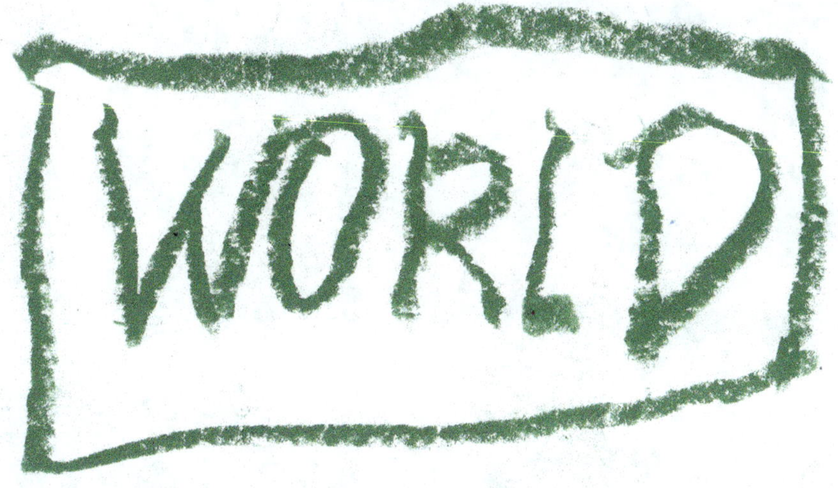

POSSIBILITARIAN
[WORLD]

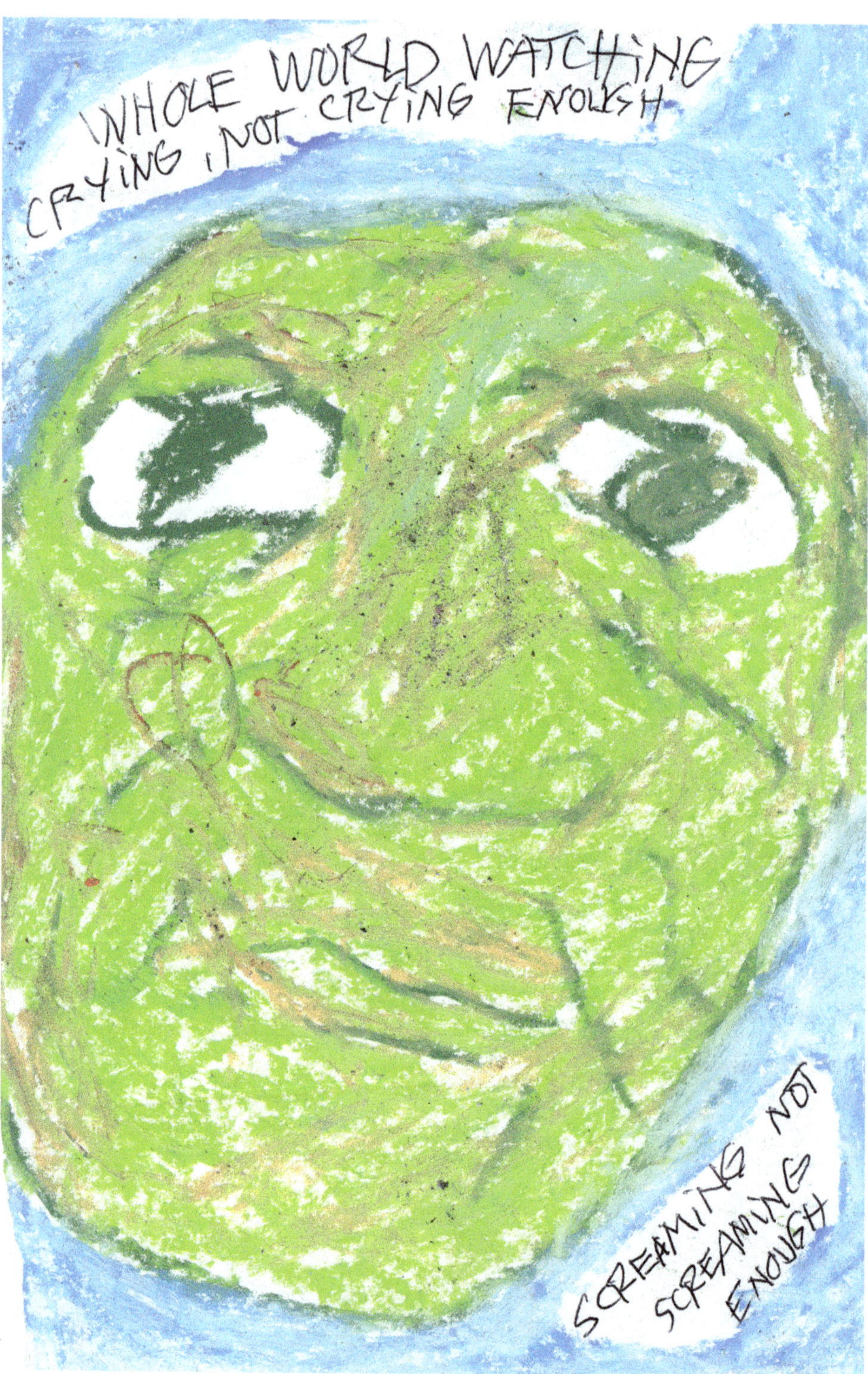

WHOLE WORLD WATCHING
CRYING, NOT CRYING ENOUGH
SCREAMING NOT SCREAMING ENOUGH

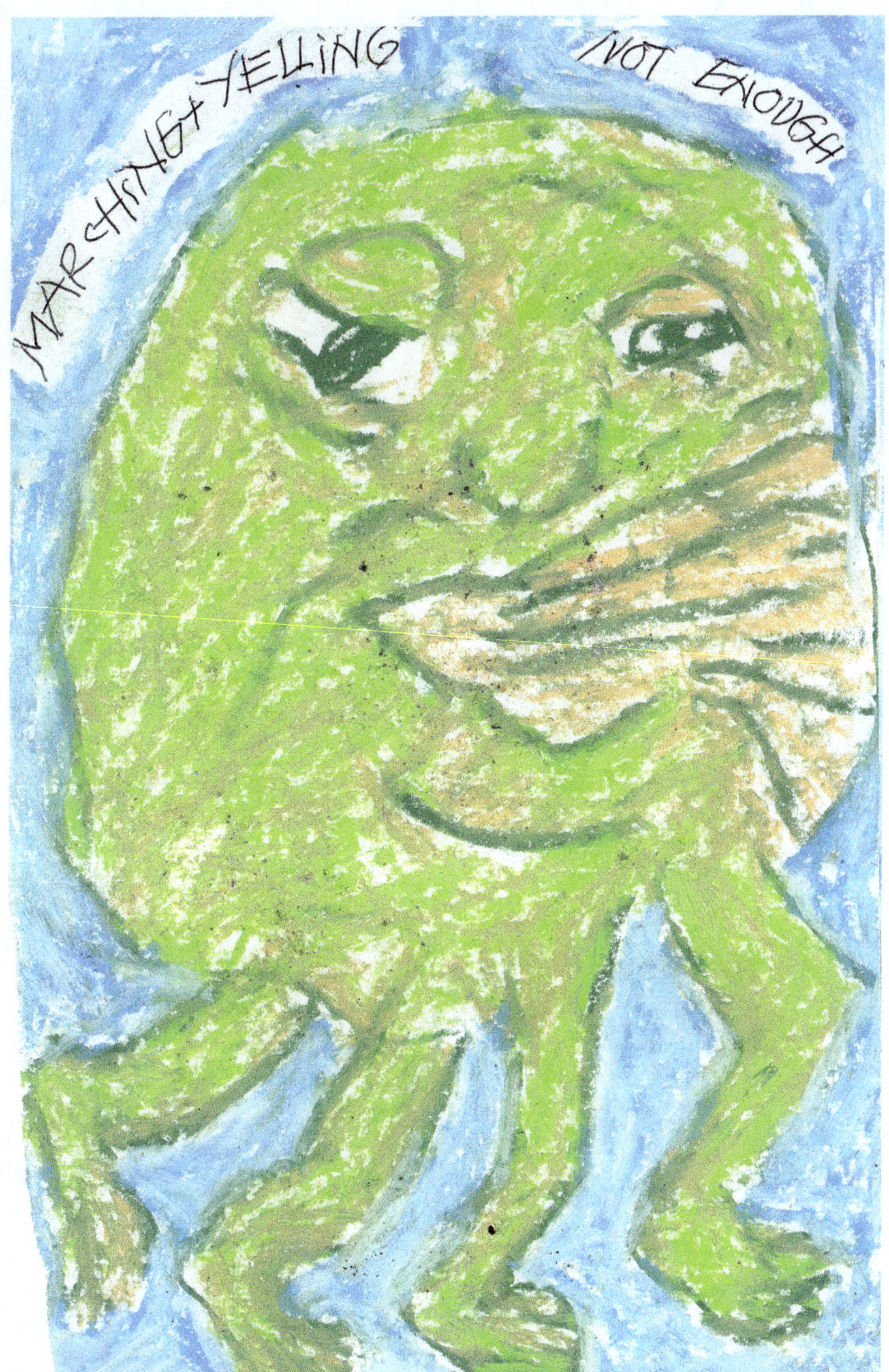

MARCHING&YELLING
NOT ENOUGH

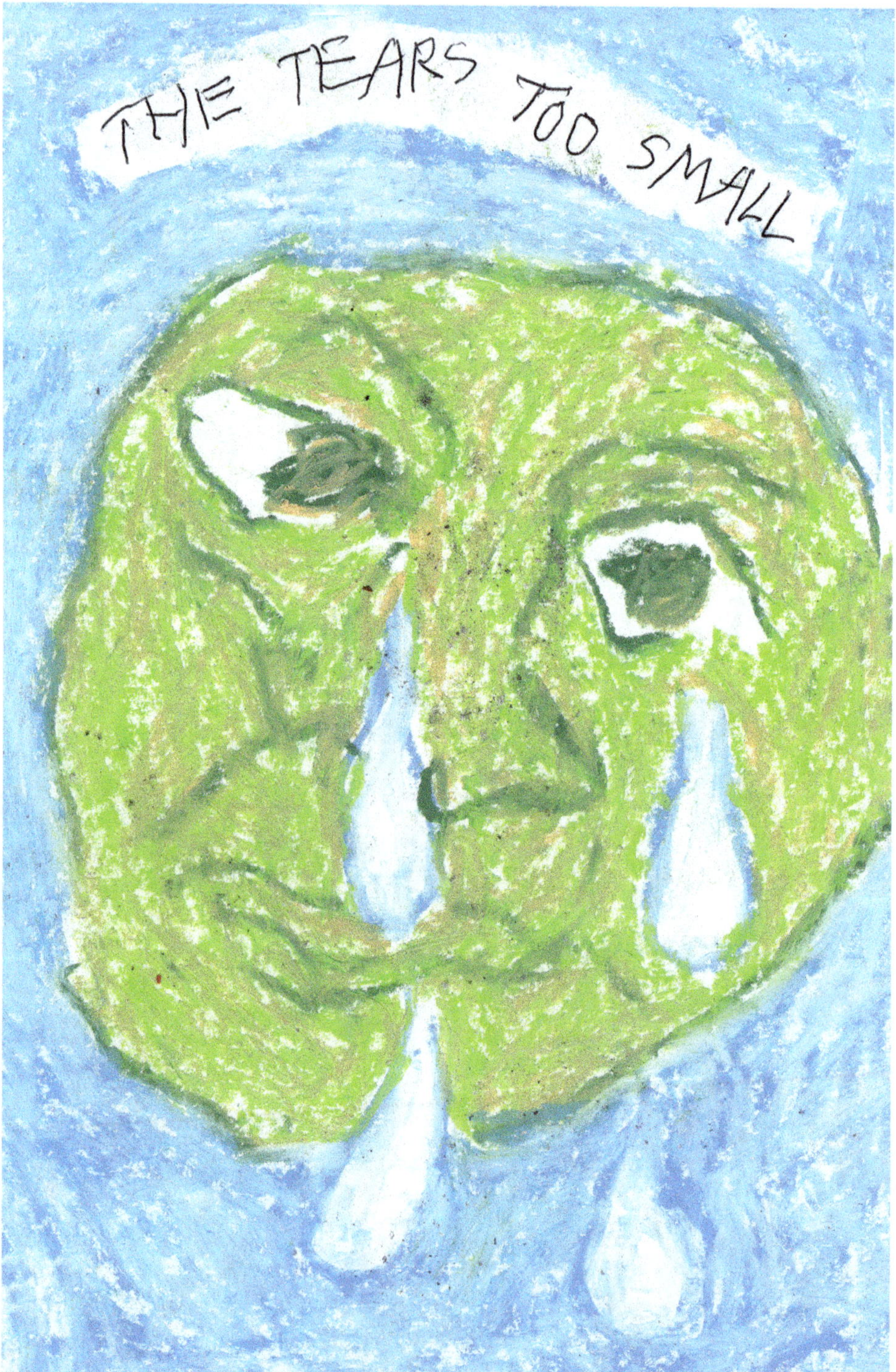

THE TEARS TOO SMALL

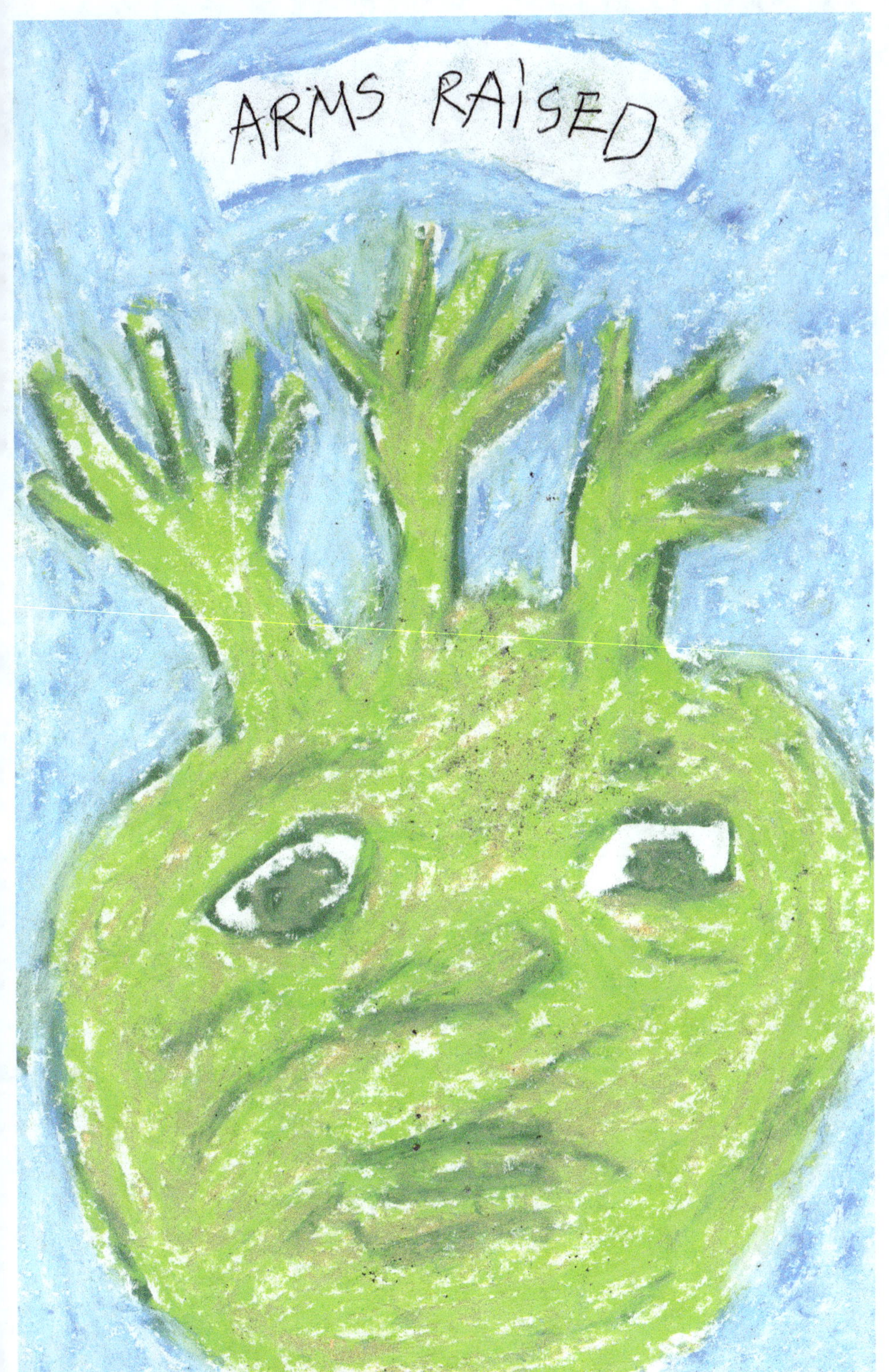
ARMS RAISED

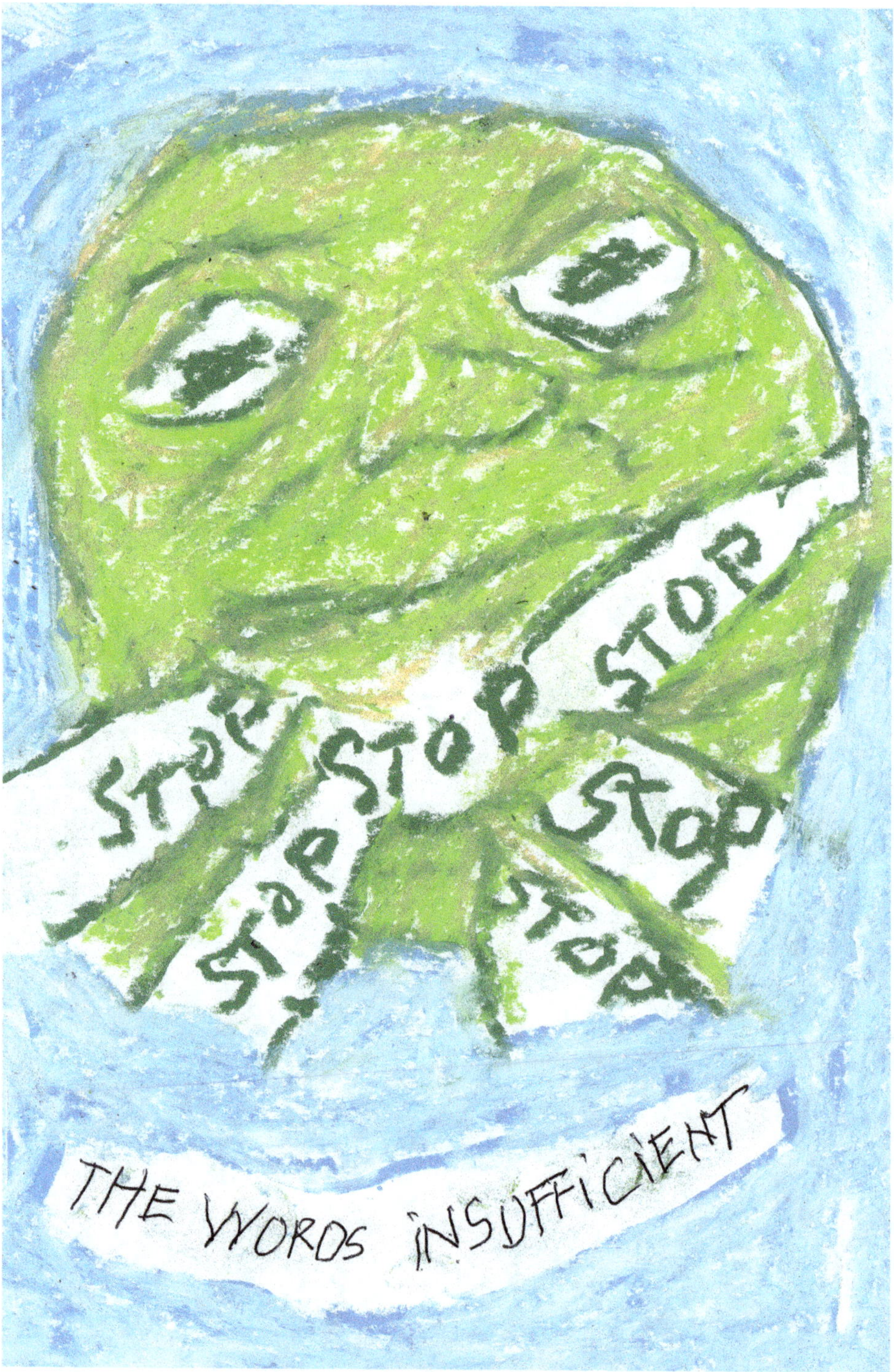

STOP
STOP
STOP
STOP
STOP
STOP
STOP
THE WORDS INSUFFICIENT

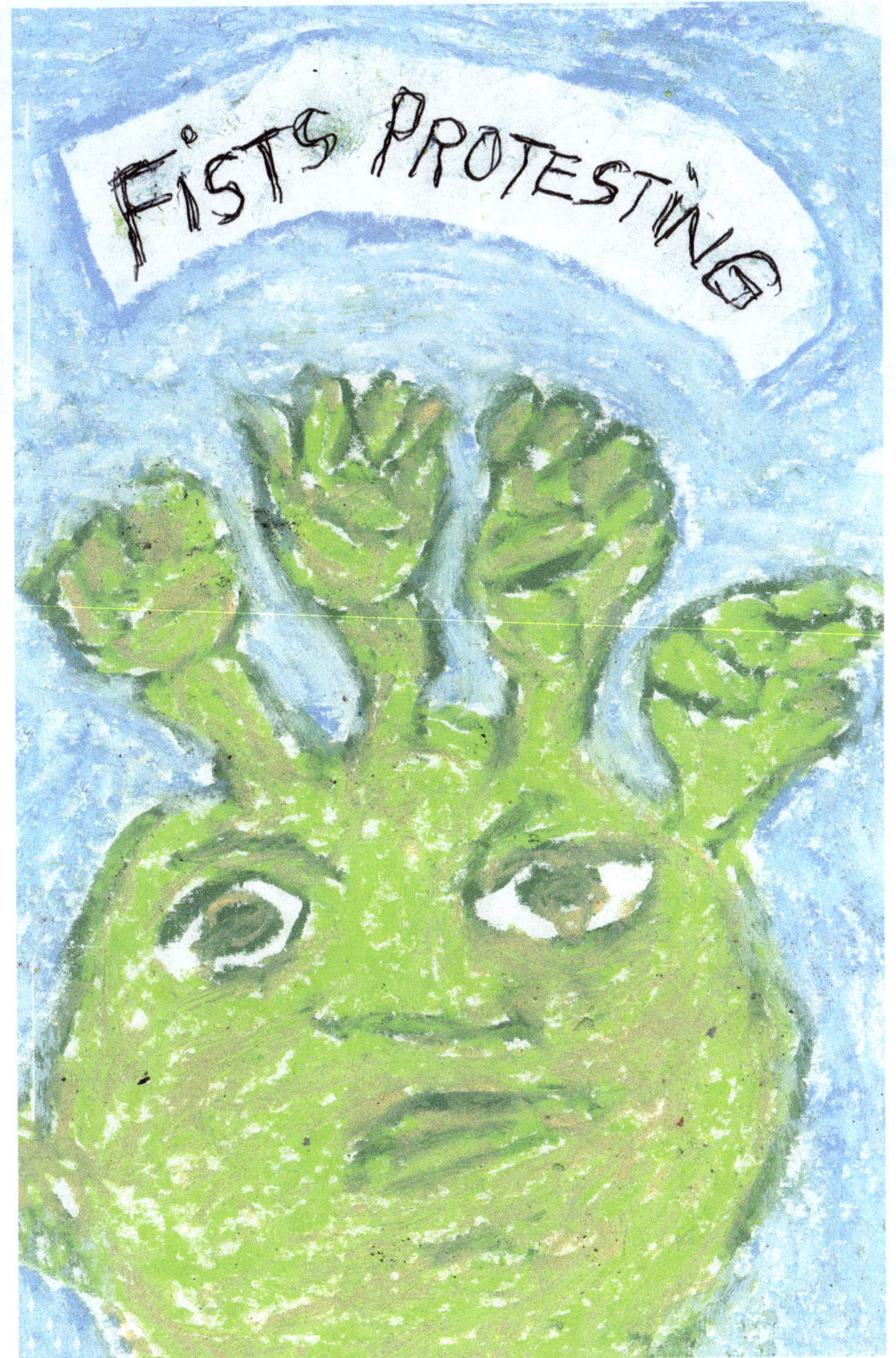
FISTS PROTESTING

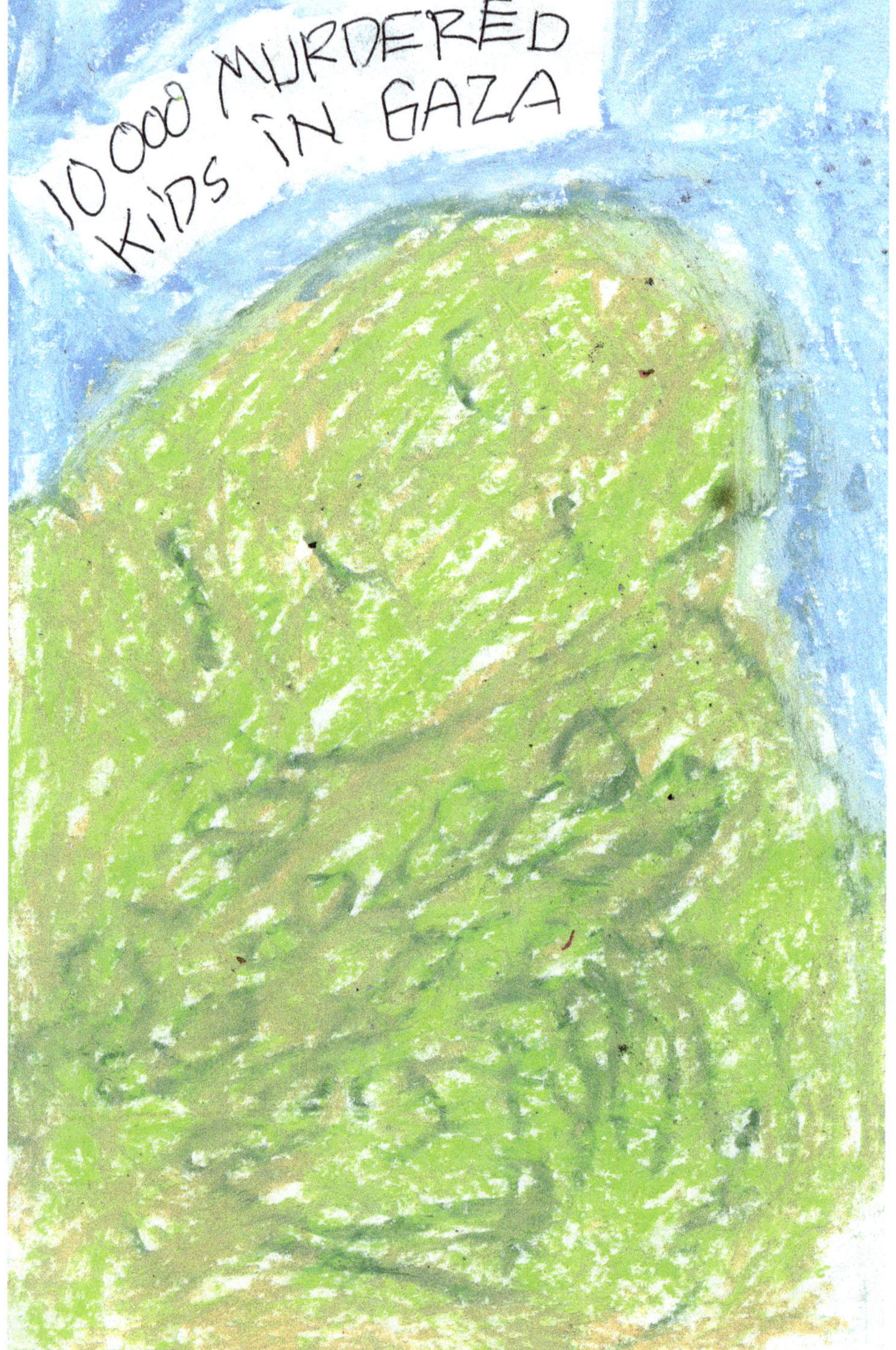

10 000 MURDERED
KIDS IN GAZA

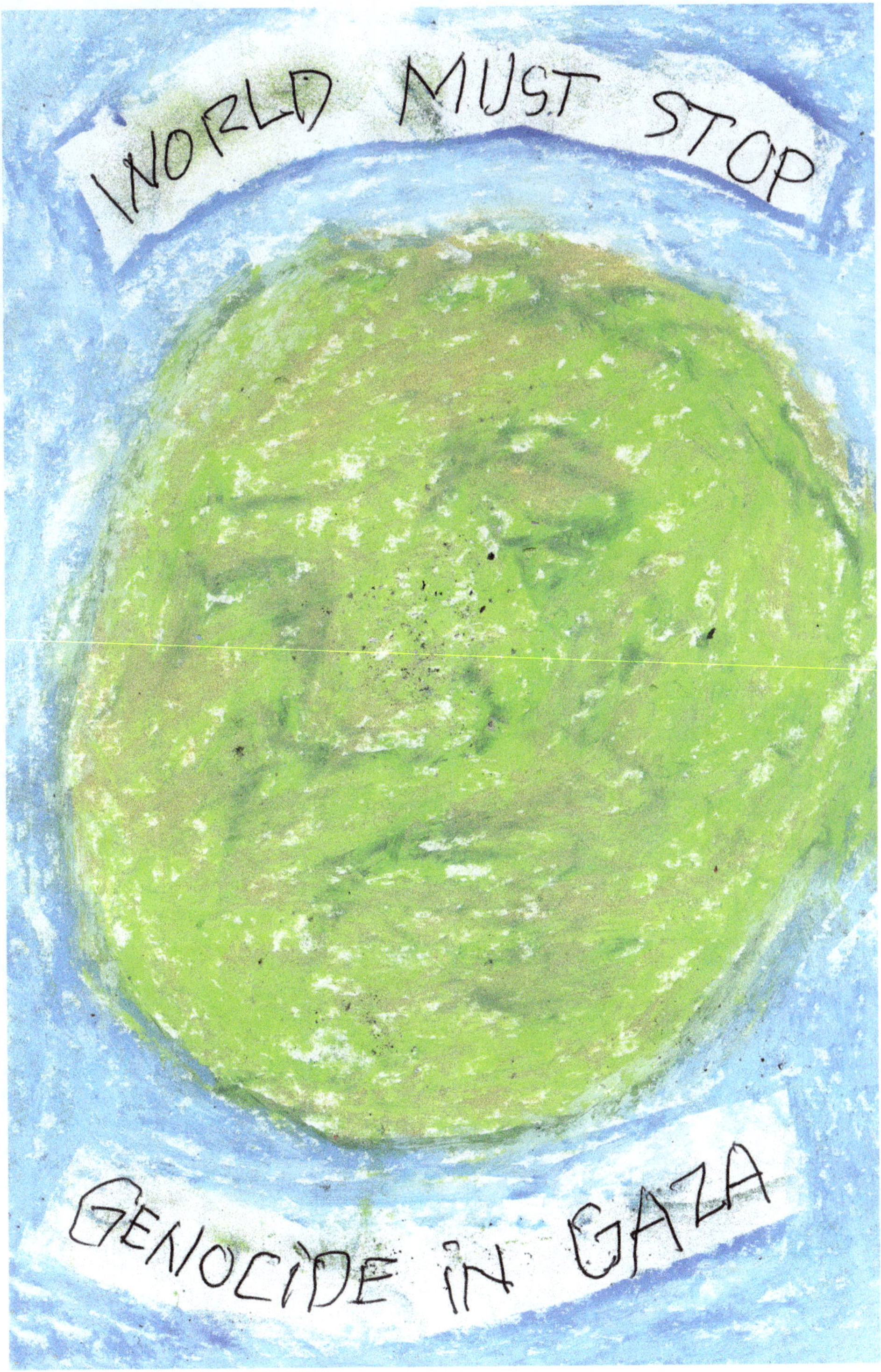

WORLD MUST STOP
GENOCIDE IN GAZA

POSSIBILITARIAN

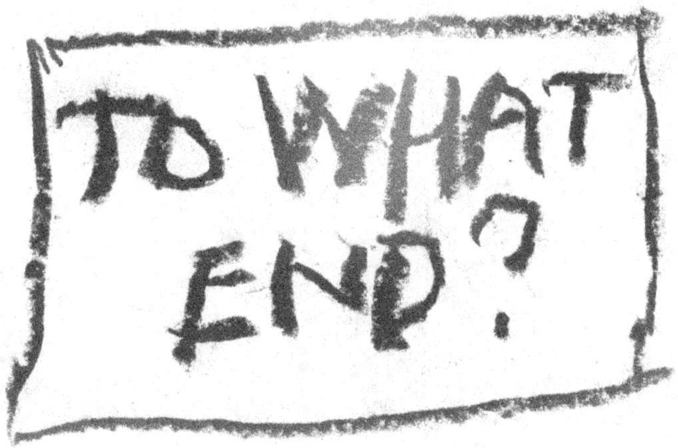

OUR LIVES FLATTENED OUT BY
MASSACRE UPON MASSACRE

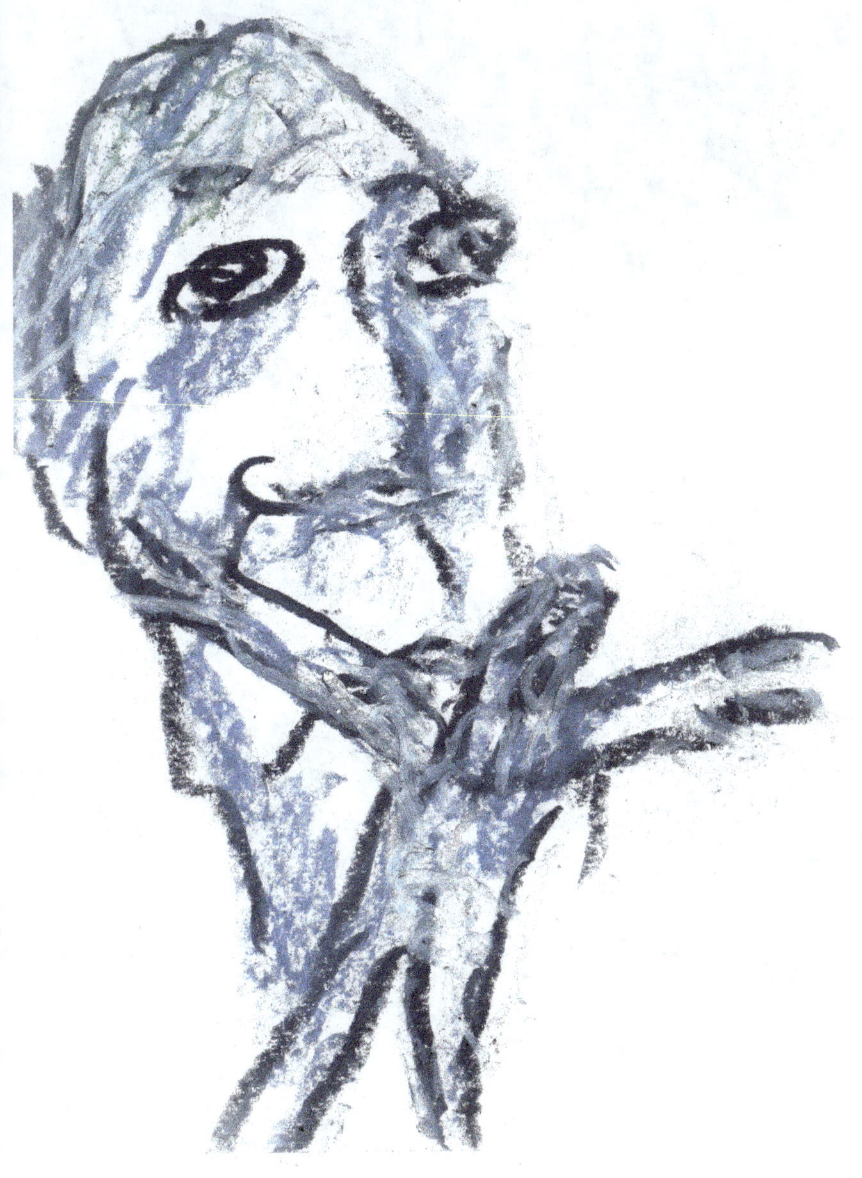

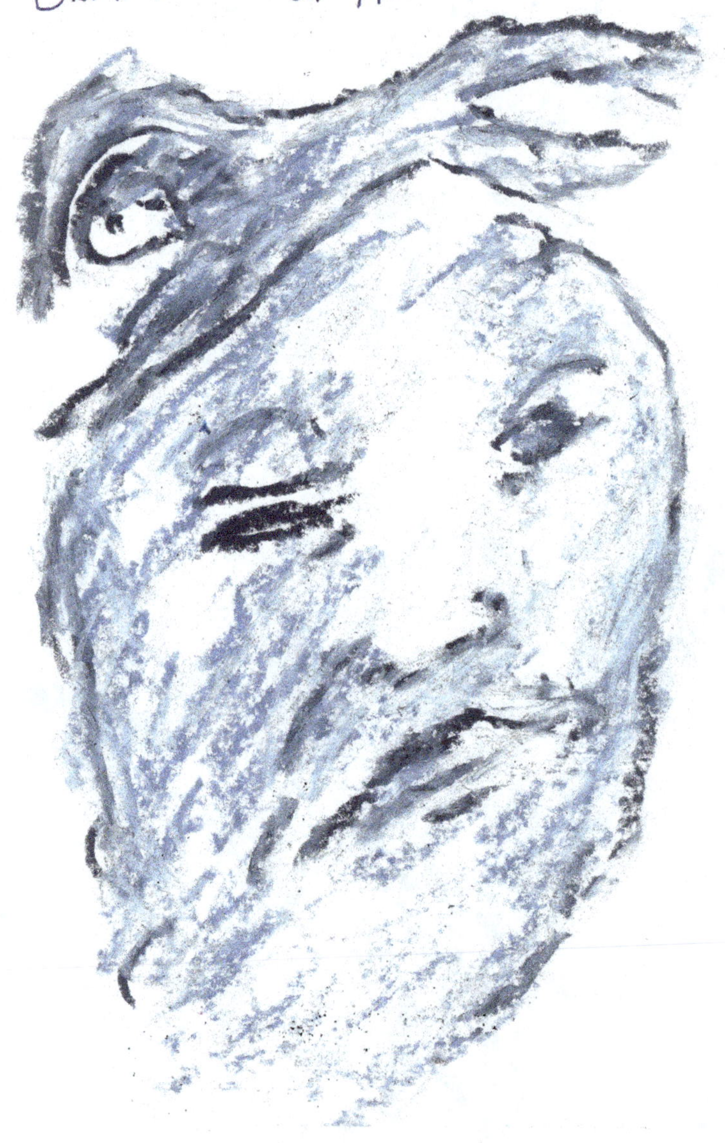

RENDERED. MEANINGLESS BY THE
QUANTITIES OF HORRORS

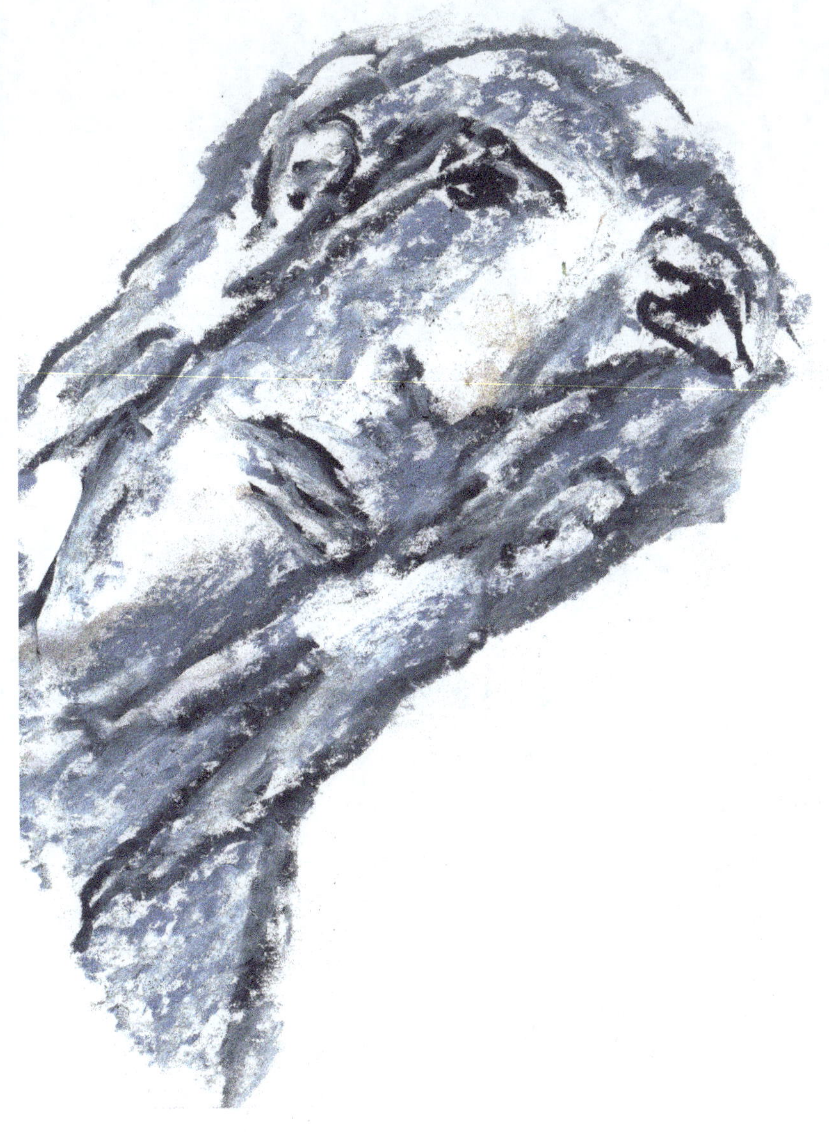

OUR OWN GUILTY WORDS
CONFRONTED WITH THE INDUSTRY
OF SHAMELESS EXTERMINATION

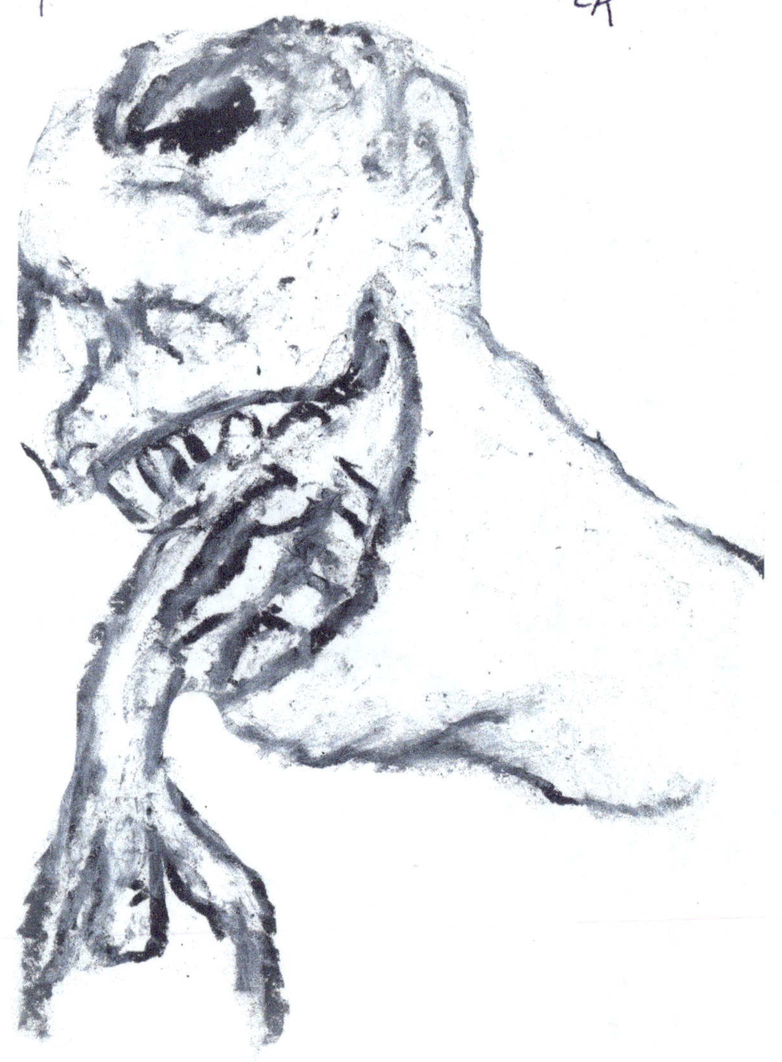

ALL OFFICES OF REPRESENTATION
THE EVIL'S LAUGHINGSTOCK

OUR DAY BY DAY LIFE
LACKING THE URGENCIES THAT
REALITY DEMANDS OF US

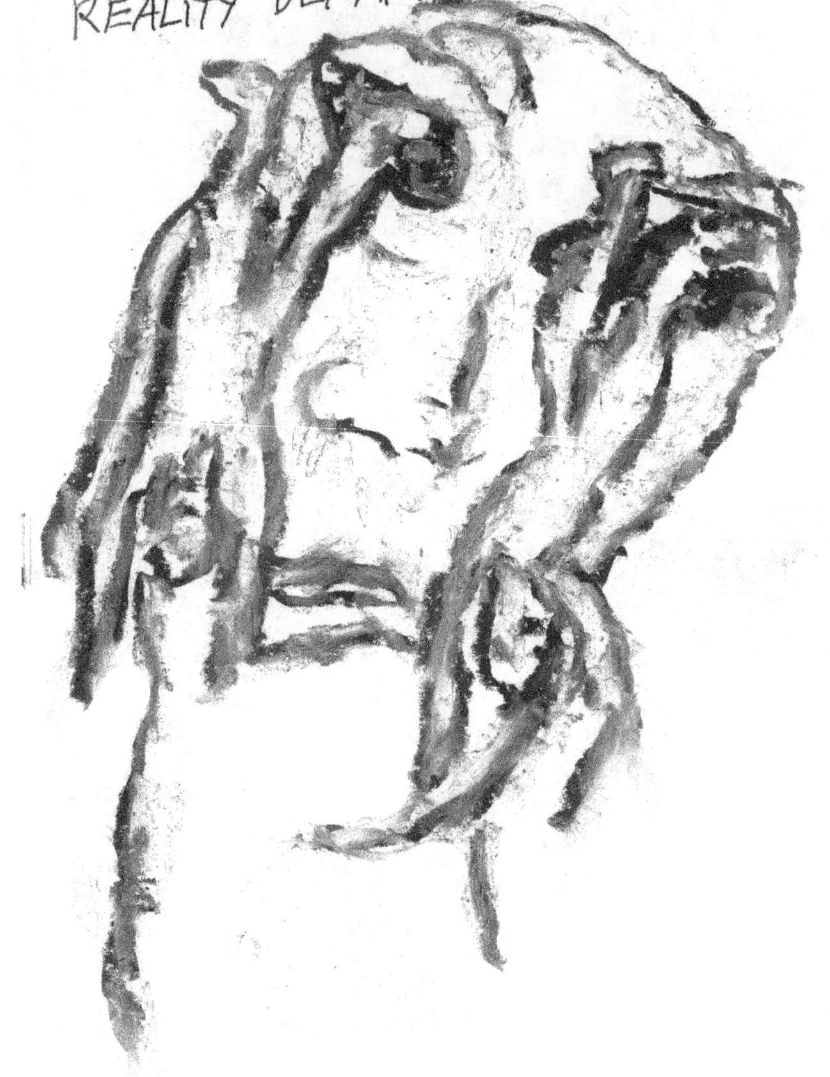

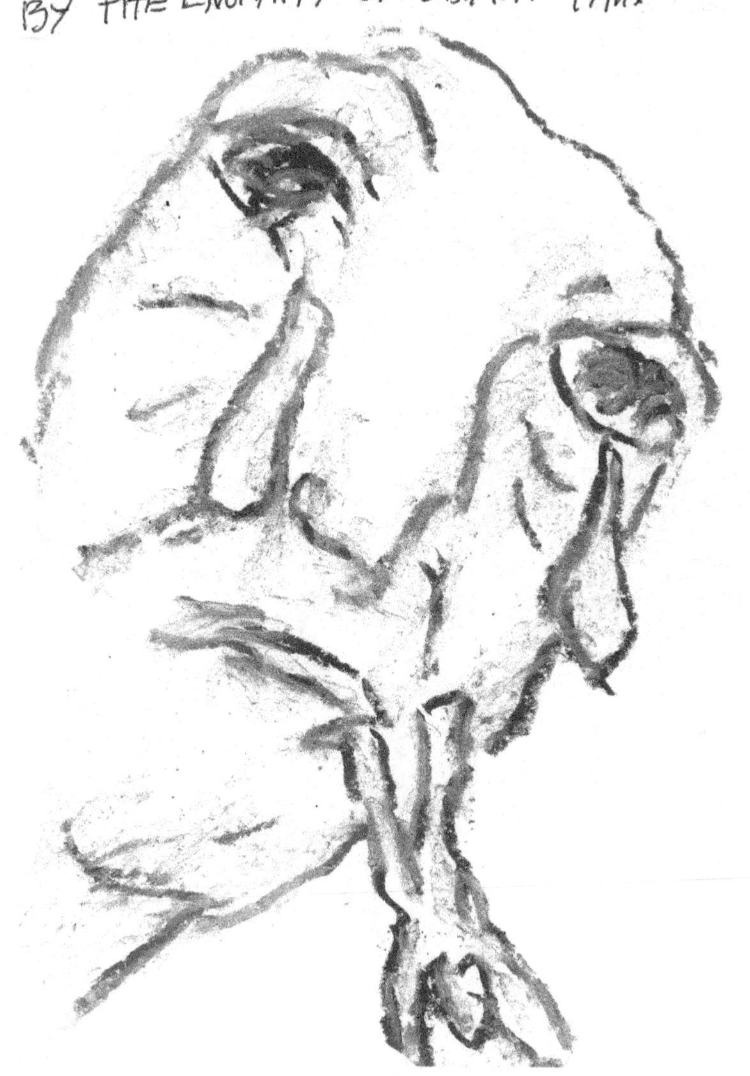
OUR OBLIGATION TO OUR ORIGINAL
EXISTENCE WHICH MIND + BODY ARE
GRANTED TO CONCEIVE BUT DEFEATED
BY THE ENORMITY OF DISTANT PAIN

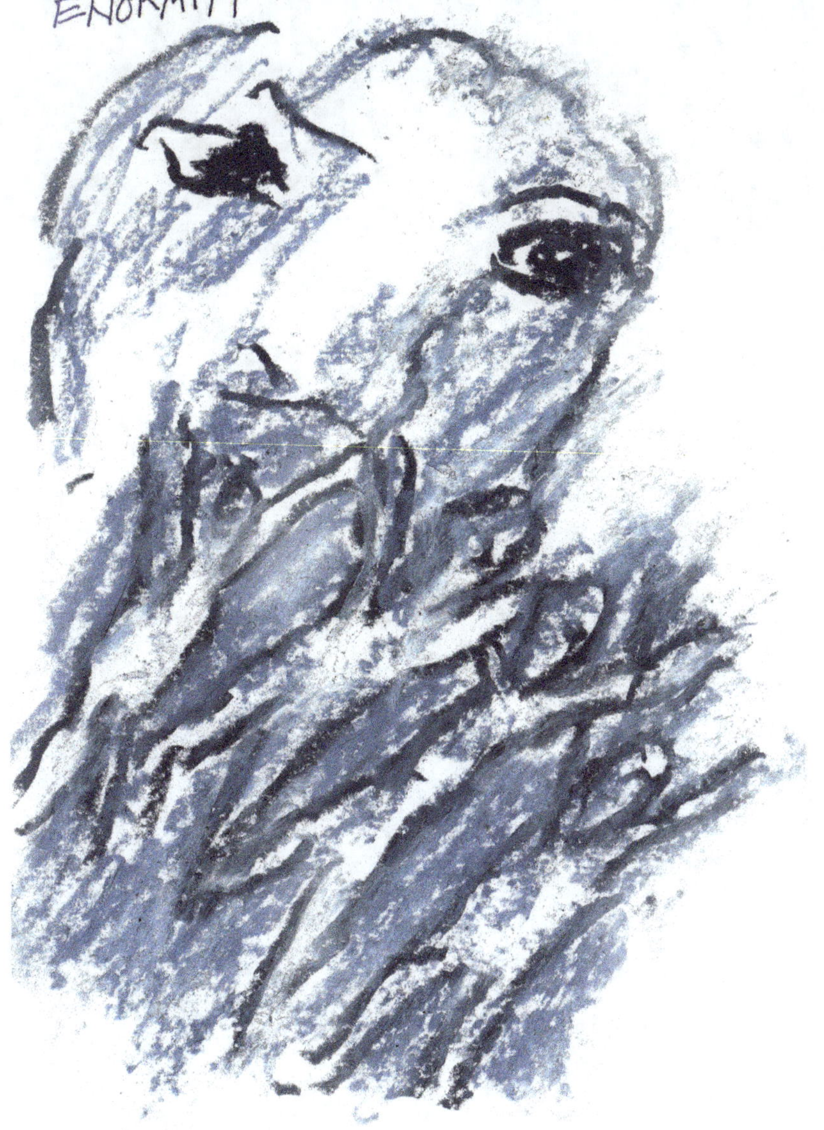
WE ARE MEANT TO DEAL WITH
BUT MADE IMPOTENT BY ITS
ENORMITY

HOW DOES THE SUN DARE
TO SHINE ON US

HOW DO OUR HANDS + FEET
PENETRATE THE EMPTY AIR
IN WHICH DIRECTION + TO
WHAT END ?

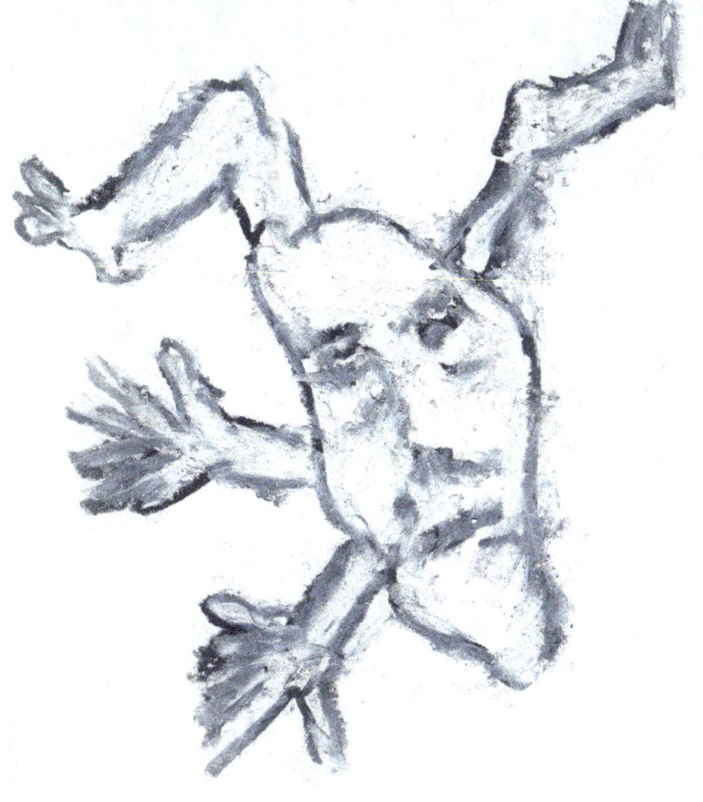

POSSIBILITARIAN

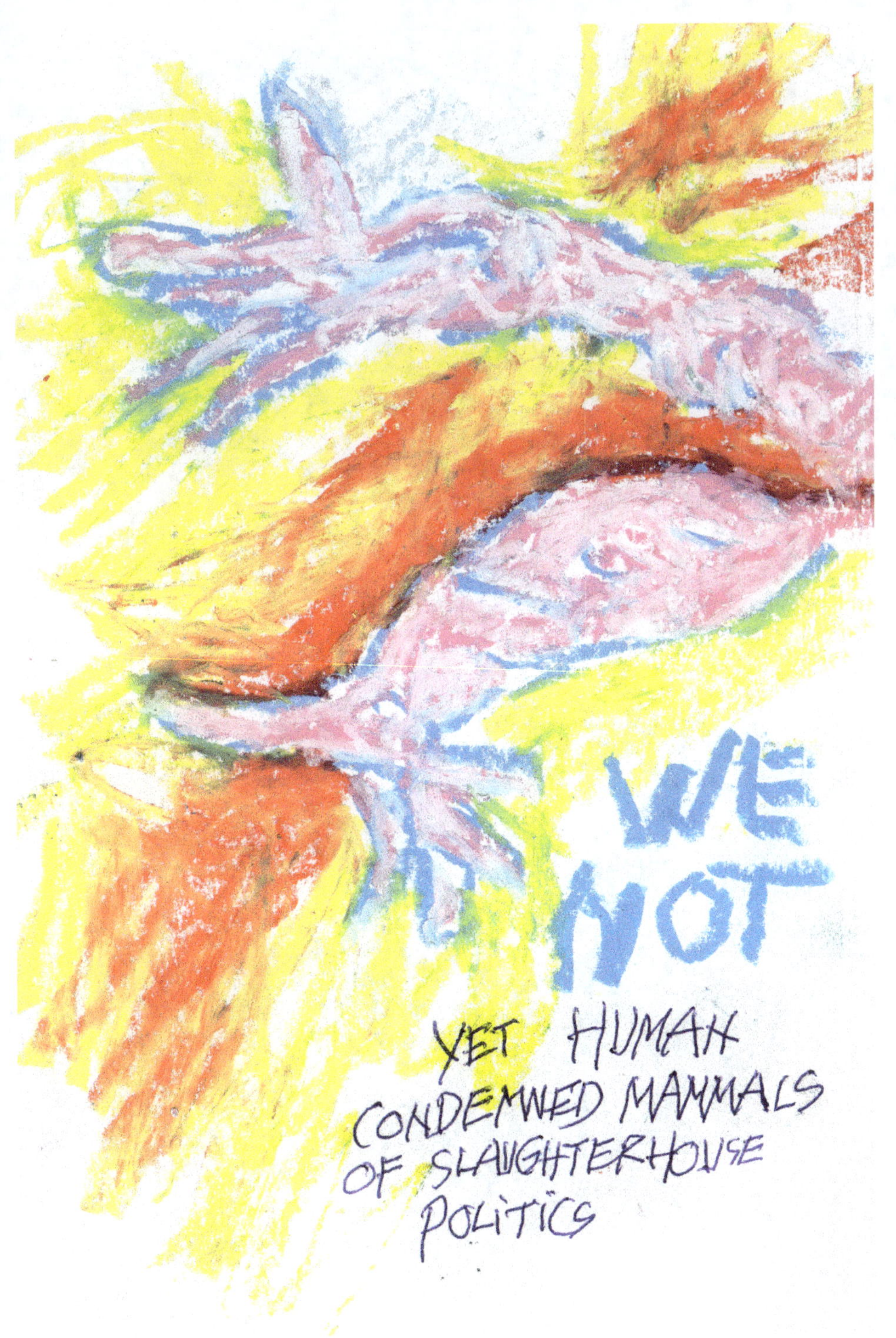

WE NOT
YET HUMAN
CONDEMNED MAMMALS
OF SLAUGHTERHOUSE
POLITICS

ARBITRARILY SELECTED
LIVING LIFE
FOR
DEATH LIFE
OR DEATH
AS IF WE WERE ALIVE
TEASED BY FUTURE
AS IF THERE WAS
FUTURE

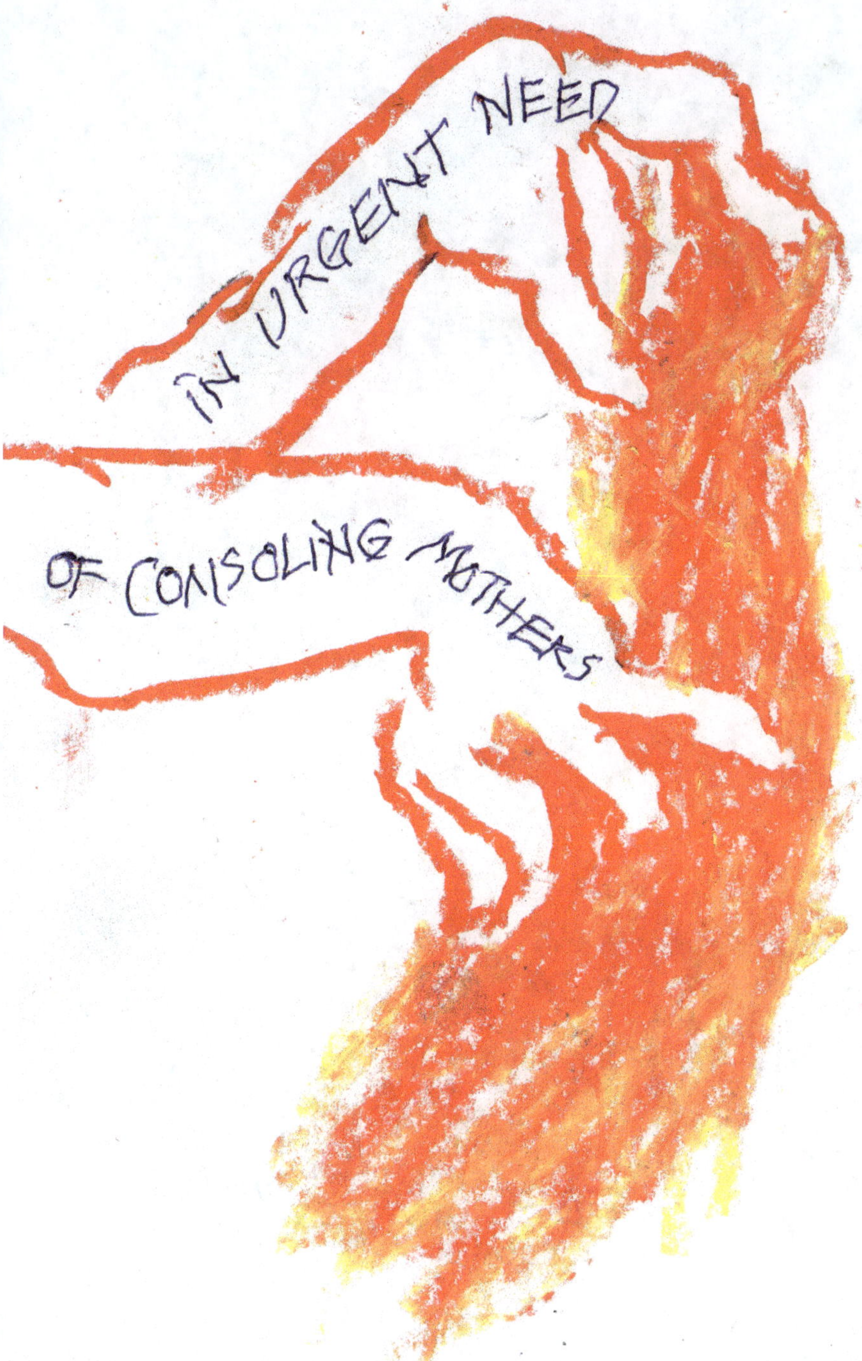

IN URGENT NEED
OF CONSOLING MOTHERS

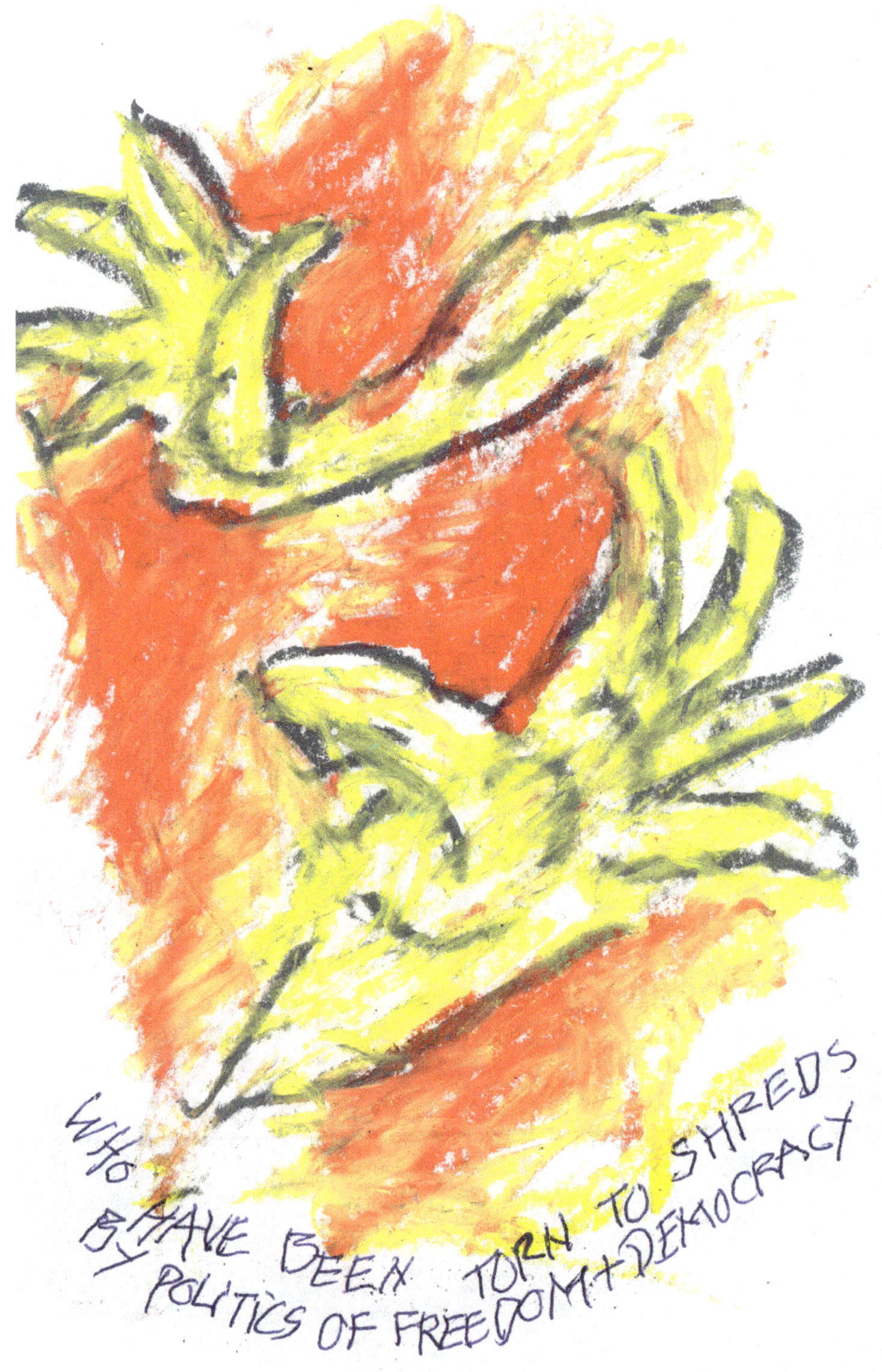

WHO HAVE BEEN TORN TO SHREDS
BY POLITICS OF FREEDOM + DEMOCRACY

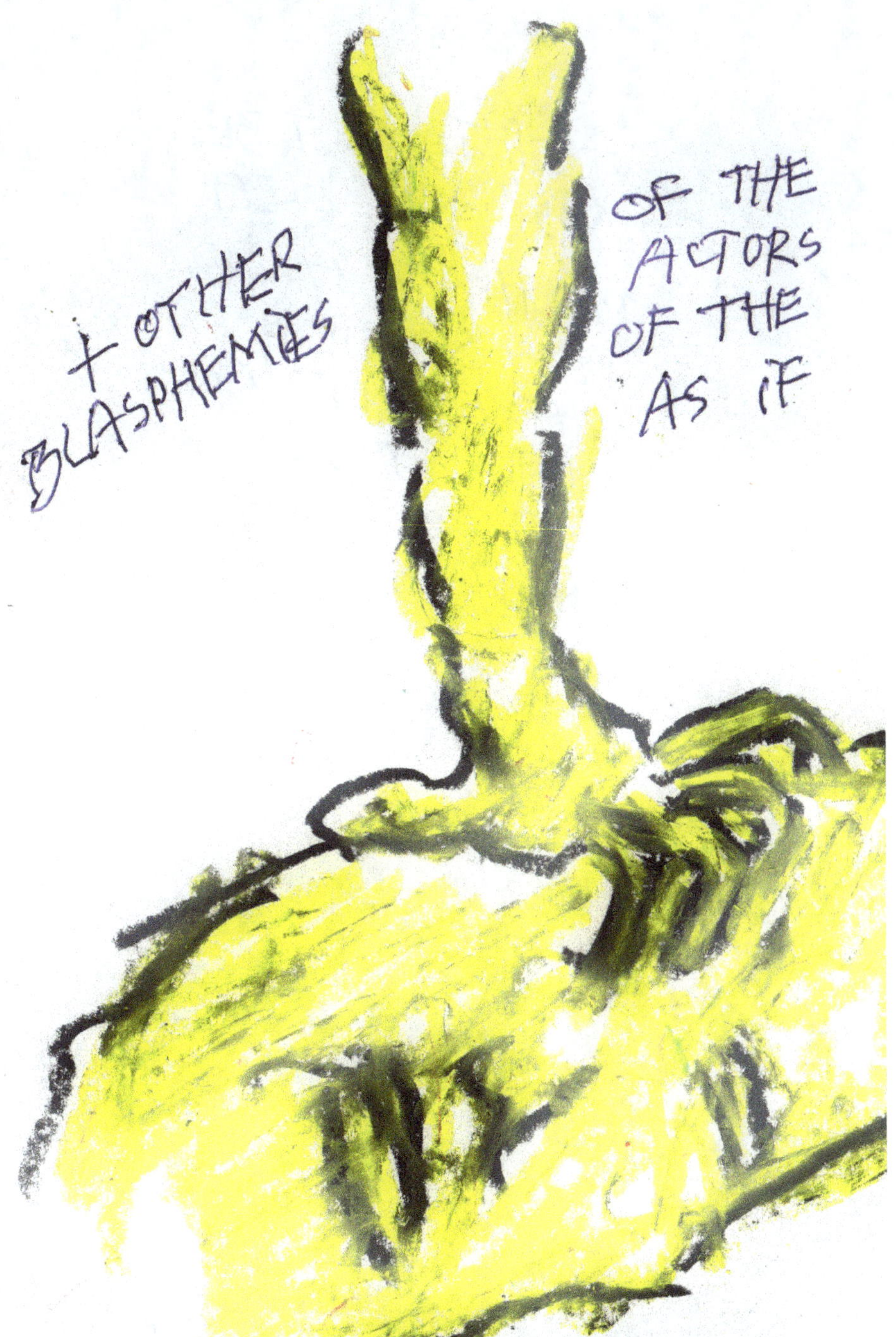
+ OTHER
BLASPHEMIES
OF THE
ACTORS
OF THE
AS IF

+ YET MUST BE
MUST NOT SLEEP
TILL HEART + MIND
FIND SOLUTIONS
WHERE THERE ARE
NONE YET ARE
OBLIGED TO THE
MUST

POSSIBILITARIAN

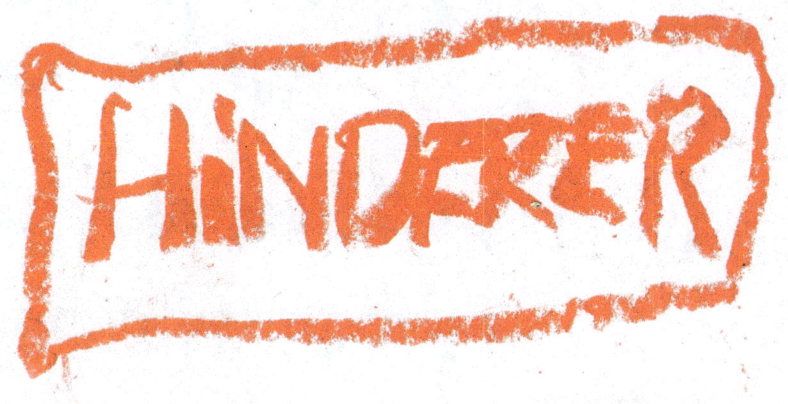

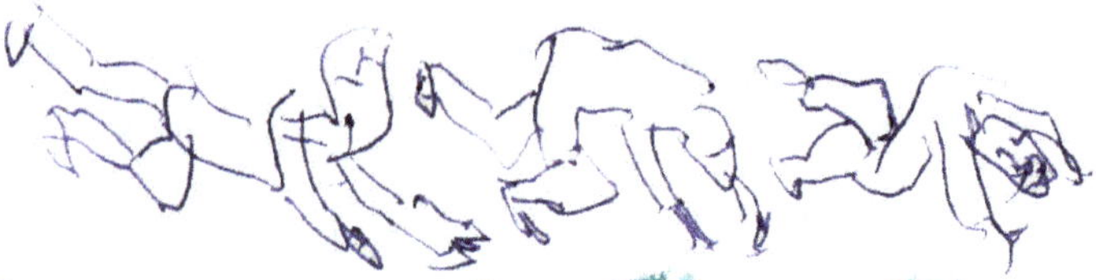

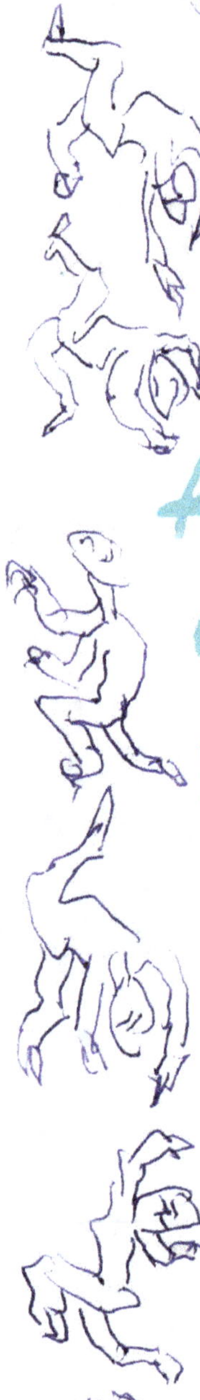

AND THE
UH + UH
+ TA-TA-TA
ON + OFF +
MORE + TA
TAH AND THE

HINDERER TORCHES
THE BASIC ELEMENTS OF
THE END THEN FALLS INTO
THE END + NEGLECTS THE
LADDERS BY HIS FEET
POINTING + TREMBLING

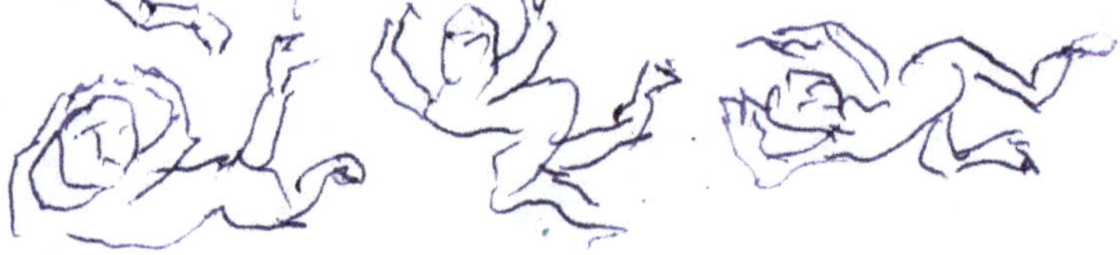

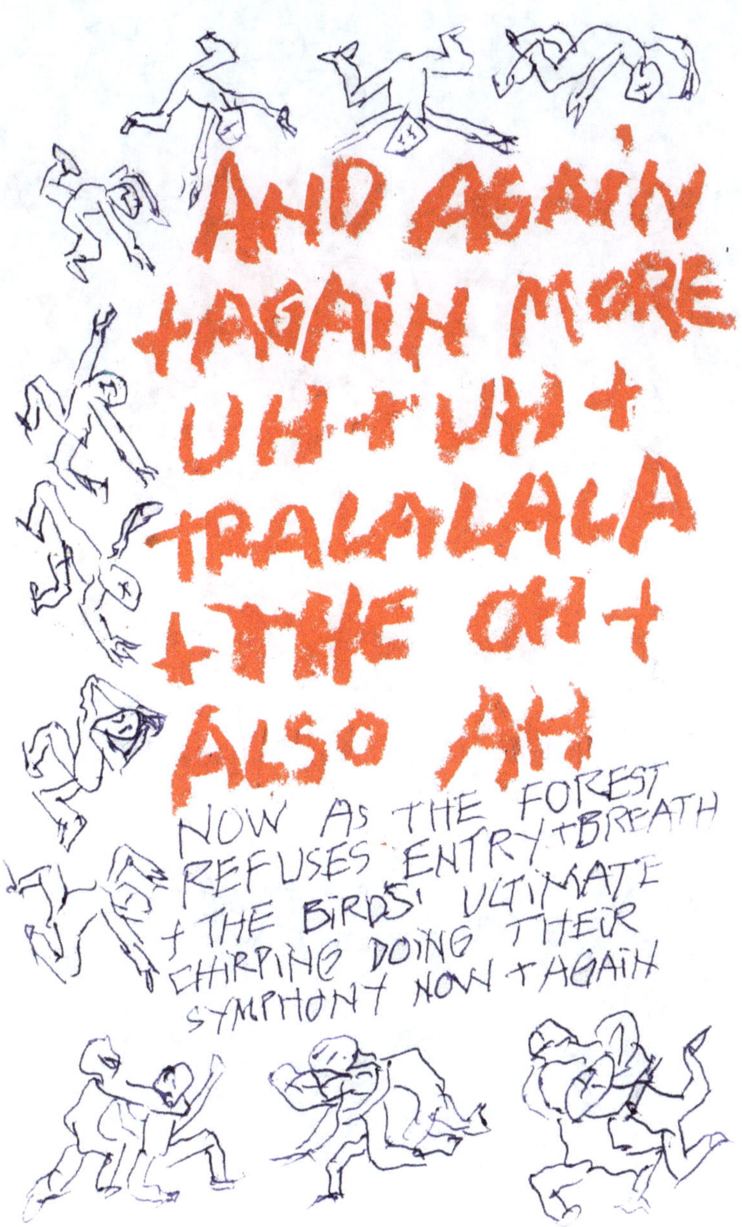

AND AGAIN
+AGAIN MORE
UH+UH+
TRALALALA
+THE OH+
ALSO AH
NOW AS THE FOREST
REFUSES ENTRY +BREATH
+THE BIRDS' ULTIMATE
CHIRPING DOING THEIR
SYMPHONY NOW +AGAIN

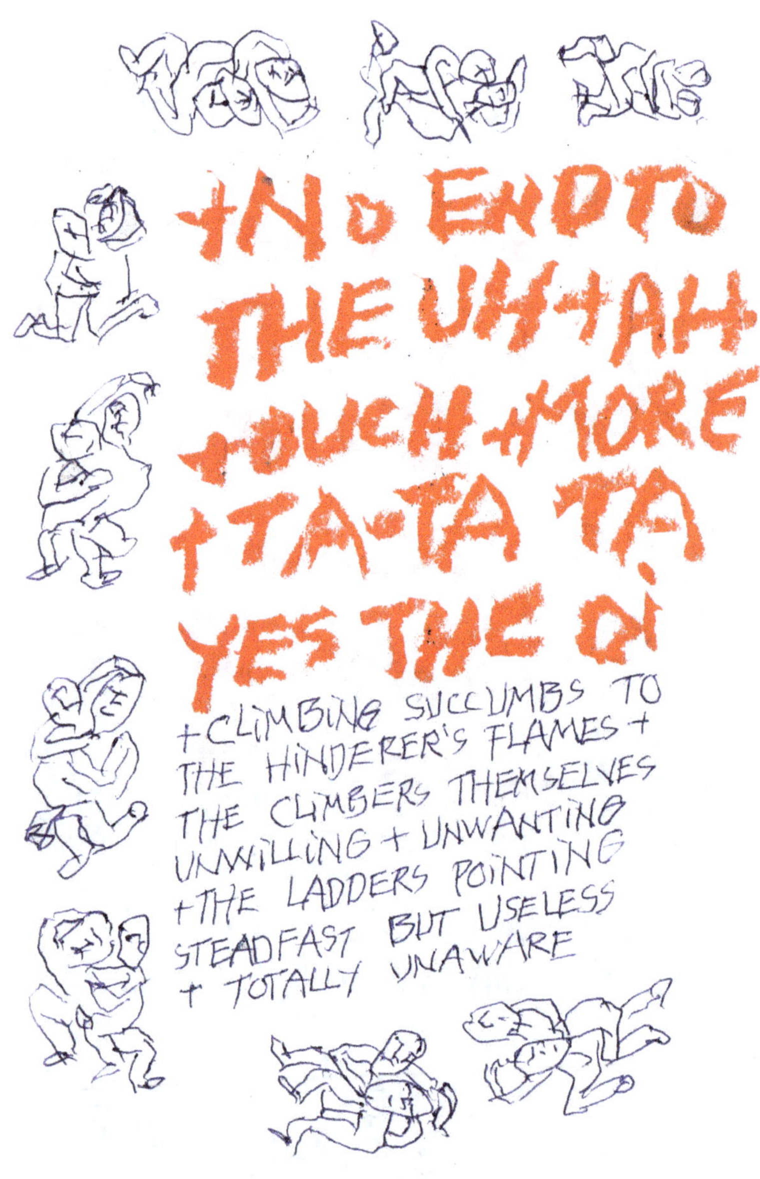

+NO END TO
THE UH+AH
+OUCH +MORE
+TA+TA TA
YES THC Qi
+CLIMBING SUCCUMBS TO
THE HINDERER'S FLAMES +
THE CLIMBERS THEMSELVES
UNWILLING + UNWANTING
+THE LADDERS POINTING
STEADFAST BUT USELESS
+ TOTALLY UNAWARE

+IF YOU CAN JOIN THE UH+ AH+ ALSO THETA TATATATA AS GOOD AS YOU CAN
THE HINDERER'S BABIES CRY VICTORY WHERE THERE IS NONE WITHOUT CLIMBING+ WANTING UNDER THE LADDERS

WHETHER HERE OR THERE DO THE TRALA LALA LALA TOTALLY

THE LADDERS STEADFAST POINTING BUT USELESS POINT TO THE FACT THAT POINTING ITSELF IS INSUFFICIENT+MOSTLY UNWANTED+USELESS AS THE END CHIRPS+CHIRPS ANYWAY +THE PHYSICAL WORLD POINTLESS AS THE END CHIRPS ITS SYMPHONY

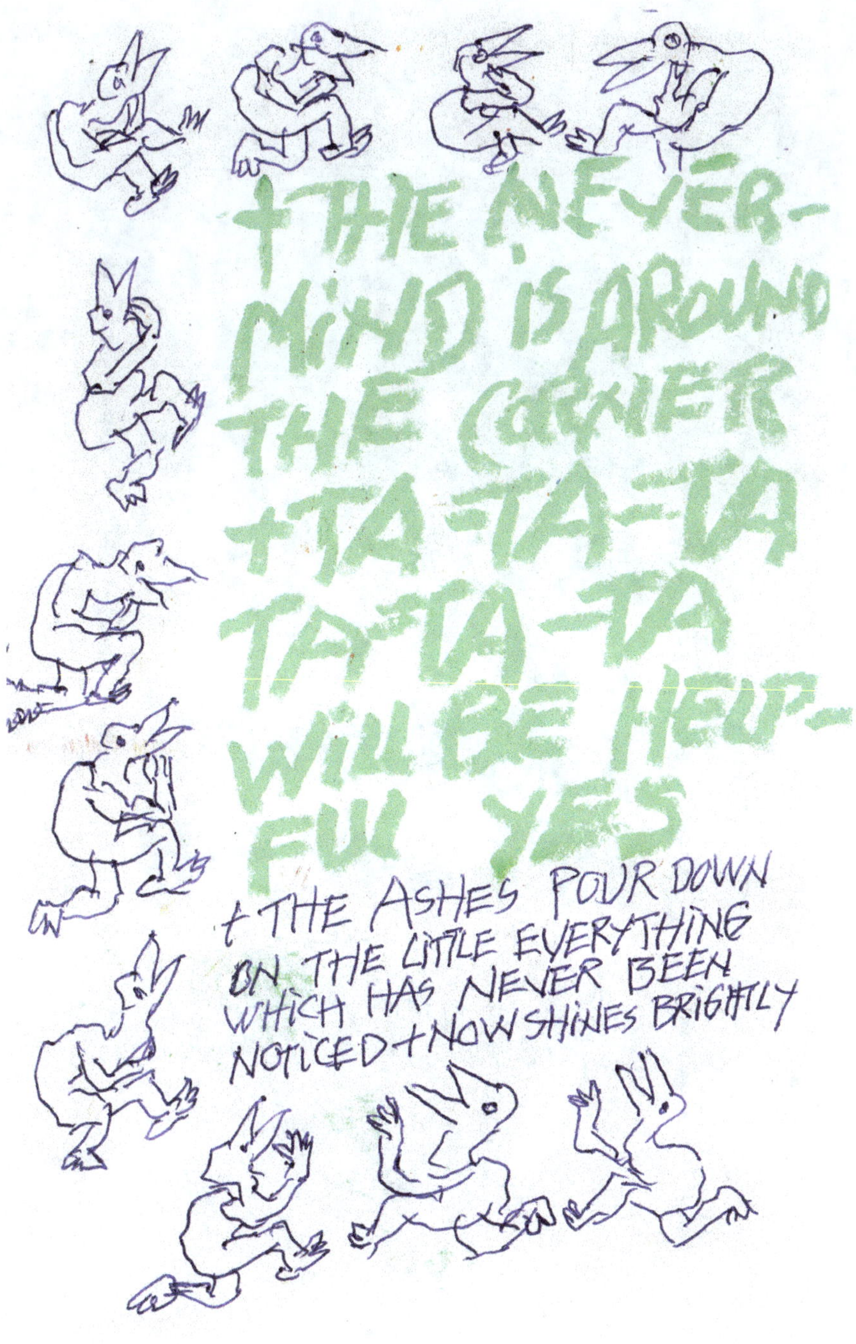
+ THE NEVER-
MIND IS AROUND
THE CORNER
+TA-TA-TA
TA-TA-TA
WILL BE HELP-
FUL YES
+ THE ASHES POUR DOWN
ON THE LITTLE EVERYTHING
WHICH HAS NEVER BEEN
NOTICED +NOW SHINES BRIGHTLY

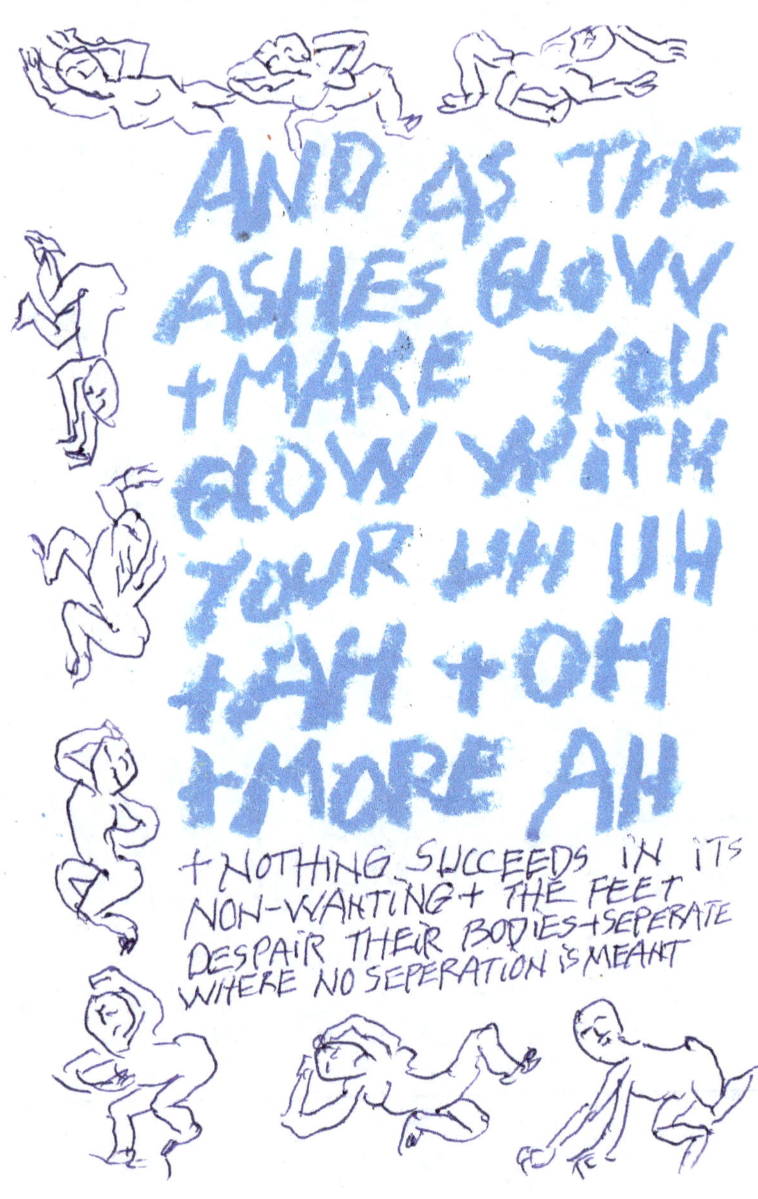

AND AS THE ASHES GLOW + MAKE YOU GLOW WITH YOUR UH UH + AH + OH + MORE AH
+ NOTHING SUCCEEDS IN ITS NON-WANTING + THE FEET DESPAIR THEIR BODIES + SEPERATE WHERE NO SEPERATION IS MEANT

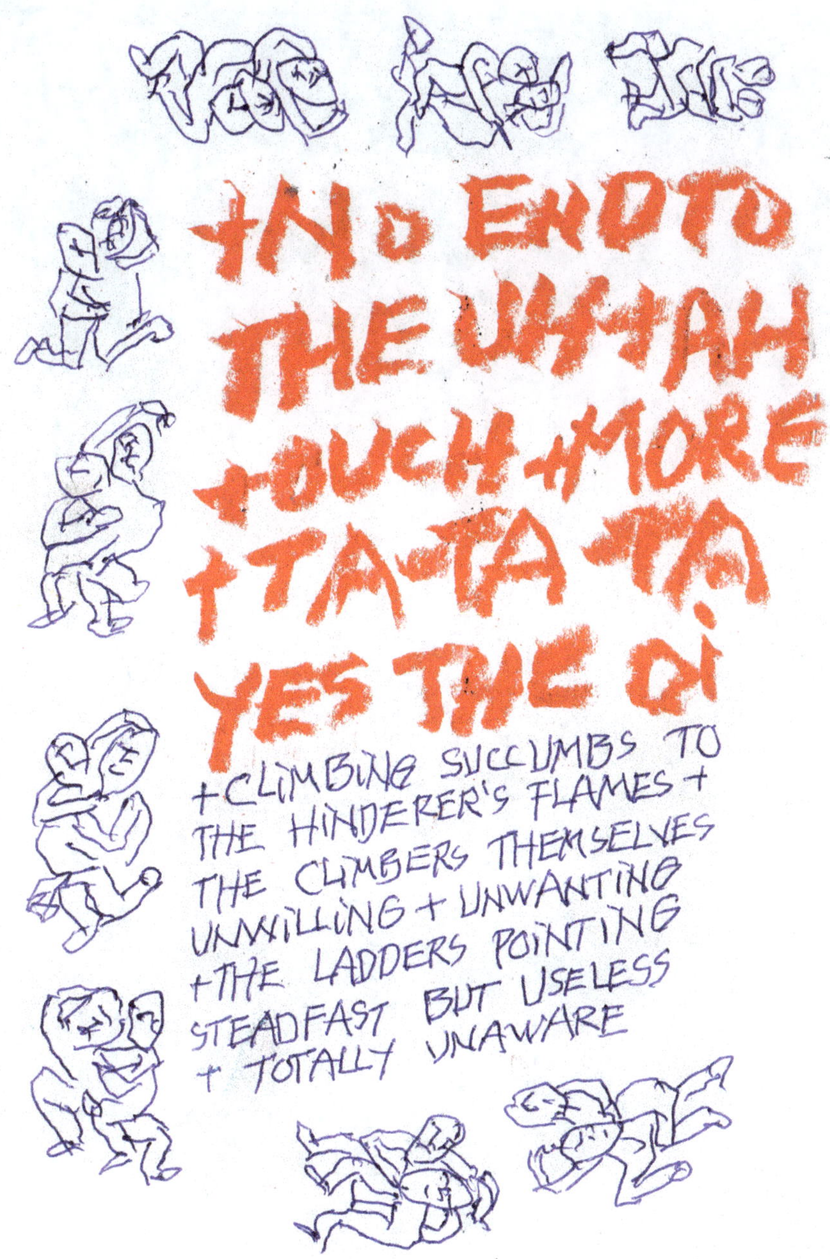
+NO ENDTO
THE UMMAH
+OUCH +MORE
+TA +TA +TA
YES THE QI
+CLIMBING SUCCUMBS TO
THE HINDERER'S FLAMES +
THE CLIMBERS THEMSELVES
UNWILLING + UNWANTING
+THE LADDERS POINTING
STEADFAST BUT USELESS
+ TOTALLY UNAWARE

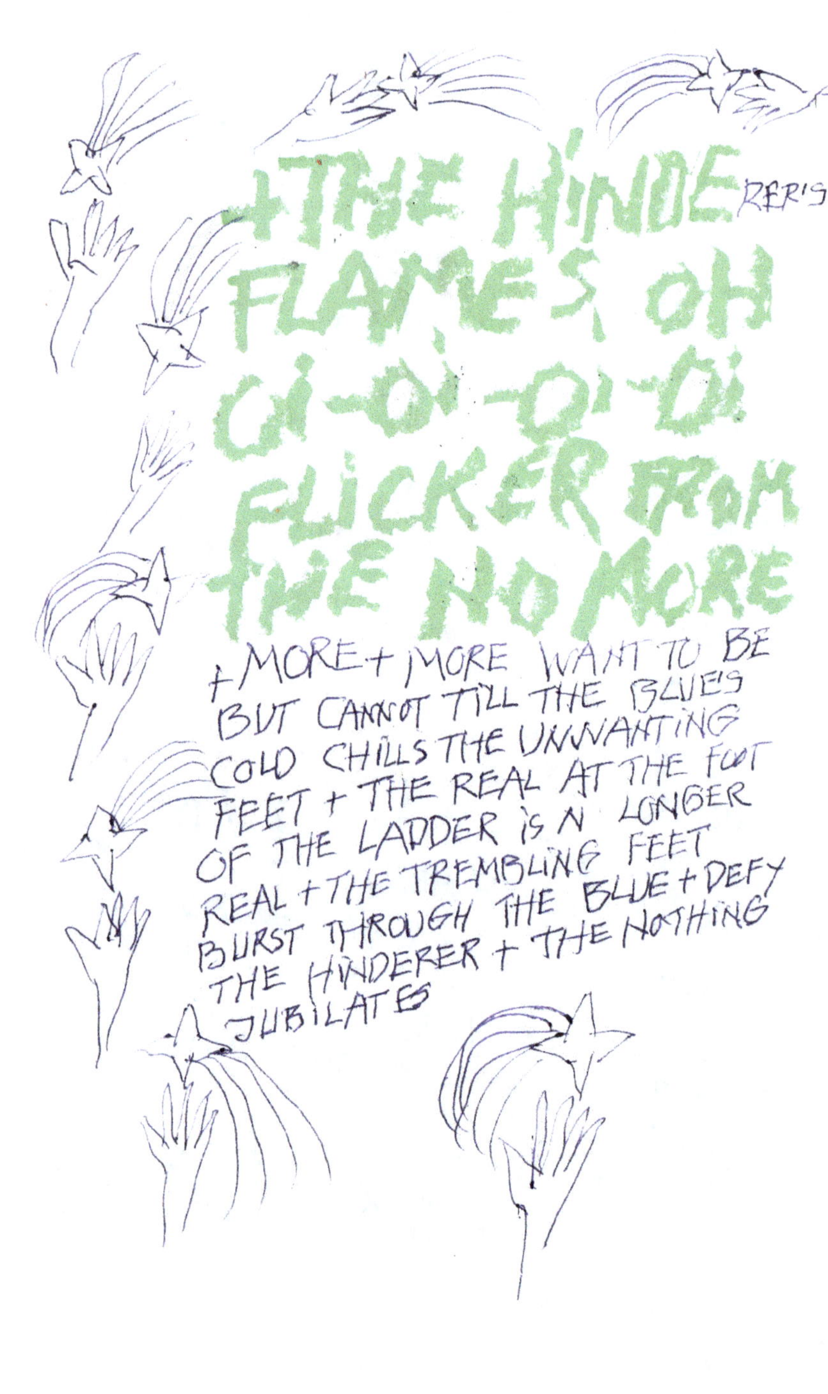
+ THE HINDERER'S
FLAMES OH
OI-OI-OI-OI
FLICKER FROM
THE NO MORE
+ MORE + MORE WANT TO BE
BUT CANNOT TILL THE BLUE'S
COLD CHILLS THE UNWANTING
FEET + THE REAL AT THE FOOT
OF THE LADDER IS N LONGER
REAL + THE TREMBLING FEET
BURST THROUGH THE BLUE + DEFY
THE HINDERER + THE NOTHING
JUBILATES

POSSIBILITARIAN

[OUR]

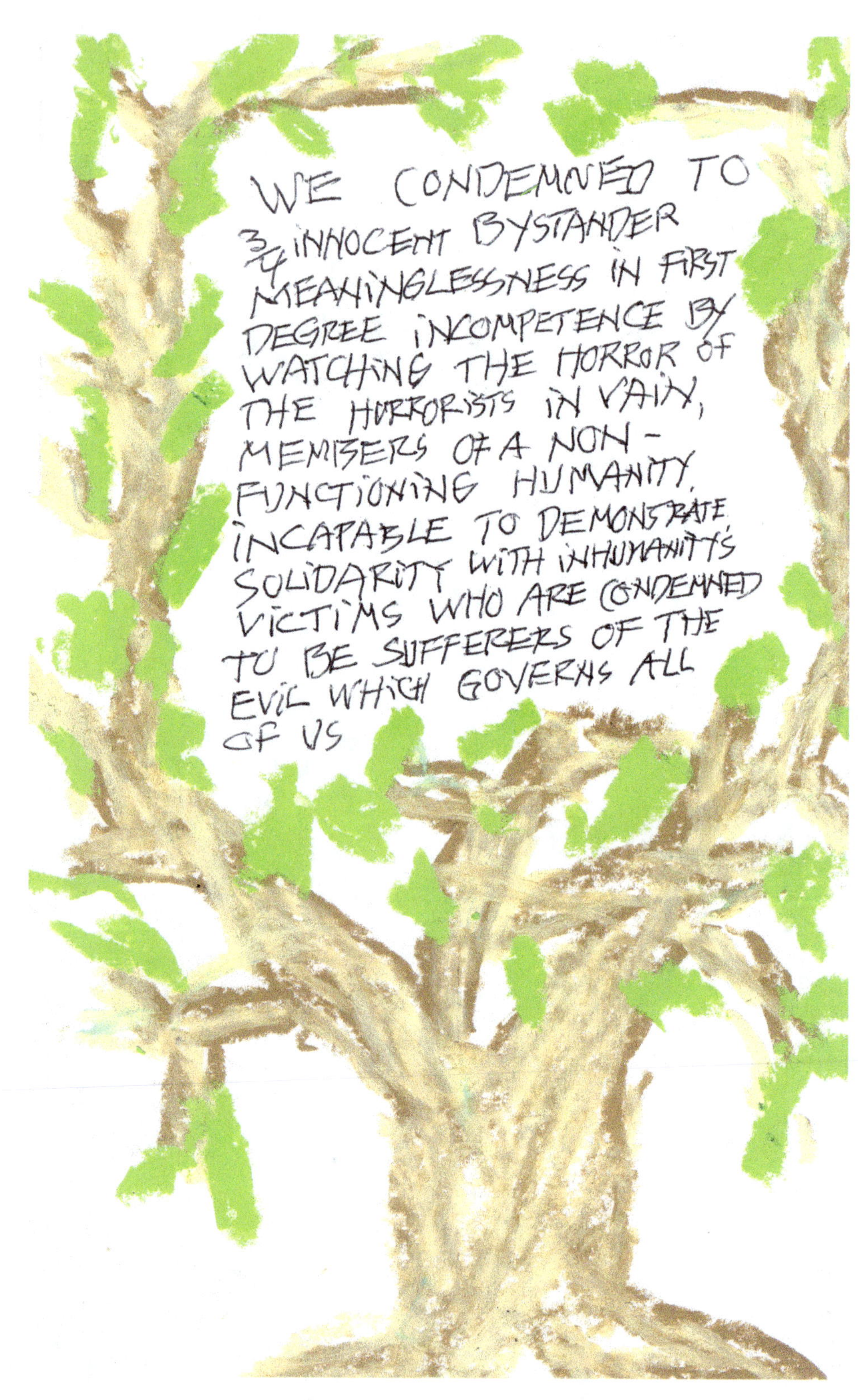

WE CONDEMNED TO
3/4 INNOCENT BYSTANDER
MEANINGLESSNESS IN FIRST
DEGREE INCOMPETENCE BY
WATCHING THE HORROR OF
THE HORRORISTS IN VAIN,
MEMBERS OF A NON-
FUNCTIONING HUMANITY,
INCAPABLE TO DEMONSTRATE
SOLIDARITY WITH INHUMANITY'S
VICTIMS WHO ARE CONDEMNED
TO BE SUFFERERS OF THE
EVIL WHICH GOVERNS ALL
OF US

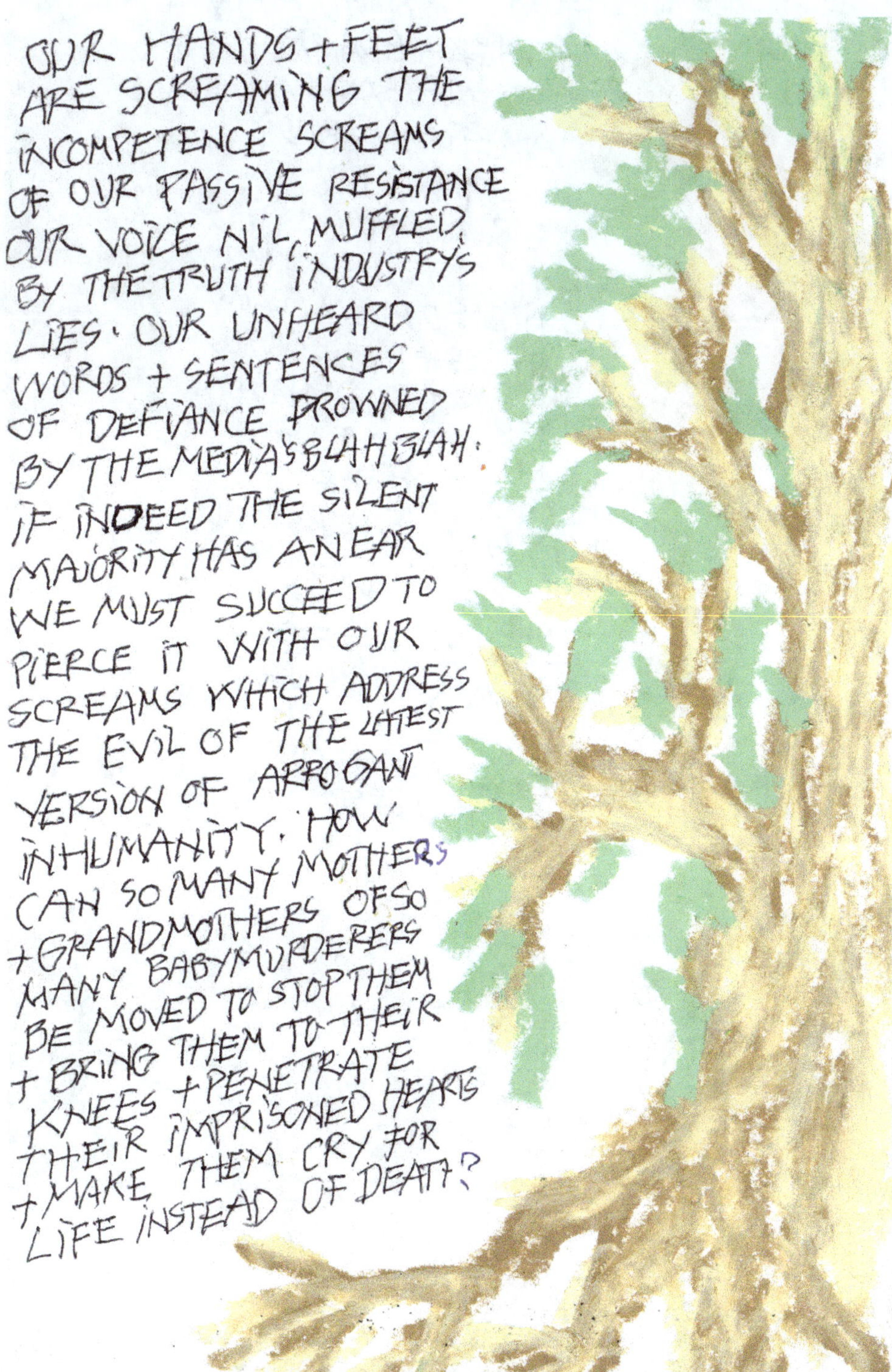

OUR HANDS + FEET
ARE SCREAMING THE
INCOMPETENCE SCREAMS
OF OUR PASSIVE RESISTANCE
OUR VOICE NIL, MUFFLED
BY THE TRUTH INDUSTRY'S
LIES. OUR UNHEARD
WORDS + SENTENCES
OF DEFIANCE DROWNED
BY THE MEDIA'S BLAH BLAH.
IF INDEED THE SILENT
MAJORITY HAS AN EAR
WE MUST SUCCEED TO
PIERCE IT WITH OUR
SCREAMS WHICH ADDRESS
THE EVIL OF THE LATEST
VERSION OF ARROGANT
INHUMANITY. HOW
CAN SO MANY MOTHERS
+ GRANDMOTHERS OF SO
MANY BABY MURDERERS
BE MOVED TO STOP THEM
+ BRING THEM TO THEIR
KNEES + PENETRATE
THEIR IMPRISONED HEARTS
+ MAKE THEM CRY FOR
LIFE INSTEAD OF DEATH?

HOW CAN SO MANY
MOTHERS + GRANDMOTHERS
OF SO MANY WEAPONS
MAKERS + EXPLOSION
SPECIALISTS LIVING
THEIR NORMAL LIVES
AS IF LIFE WAS NORMAL
WHILE SO MANY FELLOW
MOTHERS + THEIR BABIES
ARE TORTURED TO DEATH.
HOW CAN WE SONS
+ DAUGHTERS OF SO
MANY MOTHERS FEED
OUR BODIES + SOULS
WHILE OUR FELLOW
SONS + DAUGHTERS
OF SO MANY MOTHERS
ARE DEPRIVED OF
FOOD + WATER + ARE
STARVING + DESPAIRING

HOW CAN WE CONTINUE AS MEMBERS
OF A SOCIETY SO MAIMED BY EVIL, SO
NUMBED BY SO MANY ATROCITIES, SO
BLINDED BY SUCH QUANTITIES OF HORROR.
OR CAN WE EXIT OR CANCEL OUR
MEMBERSHIP IN THIS APPARENTLY
DOOMED SOCIETY. WHAT MIRACULOUS
SPARK OF HOPE CAN WE HOPE FOR IN THE
ALL-CONSUMING DARKNESS OF EVERYDAY
MORE BABIES + MOTHERS KILLED BY OUR
BABY + MOTHER KILLING SOCIETY

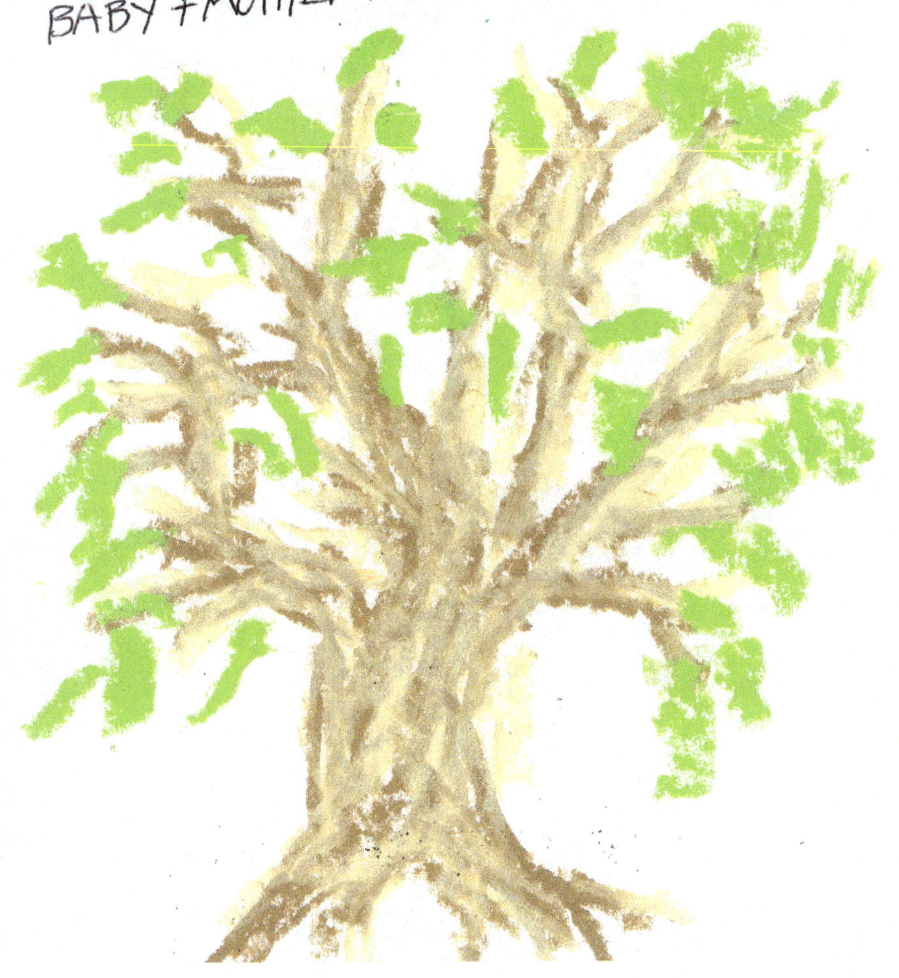

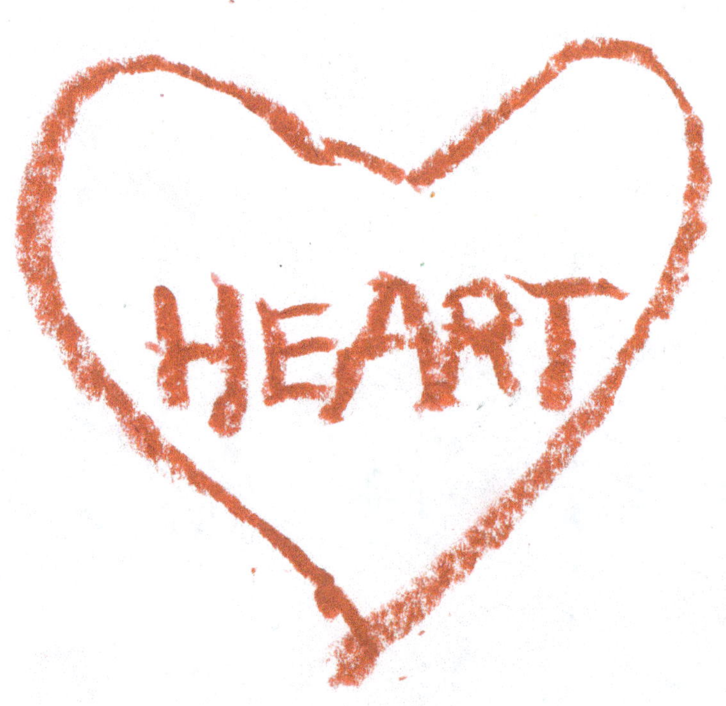

POSSIBILITARIAN
HEART

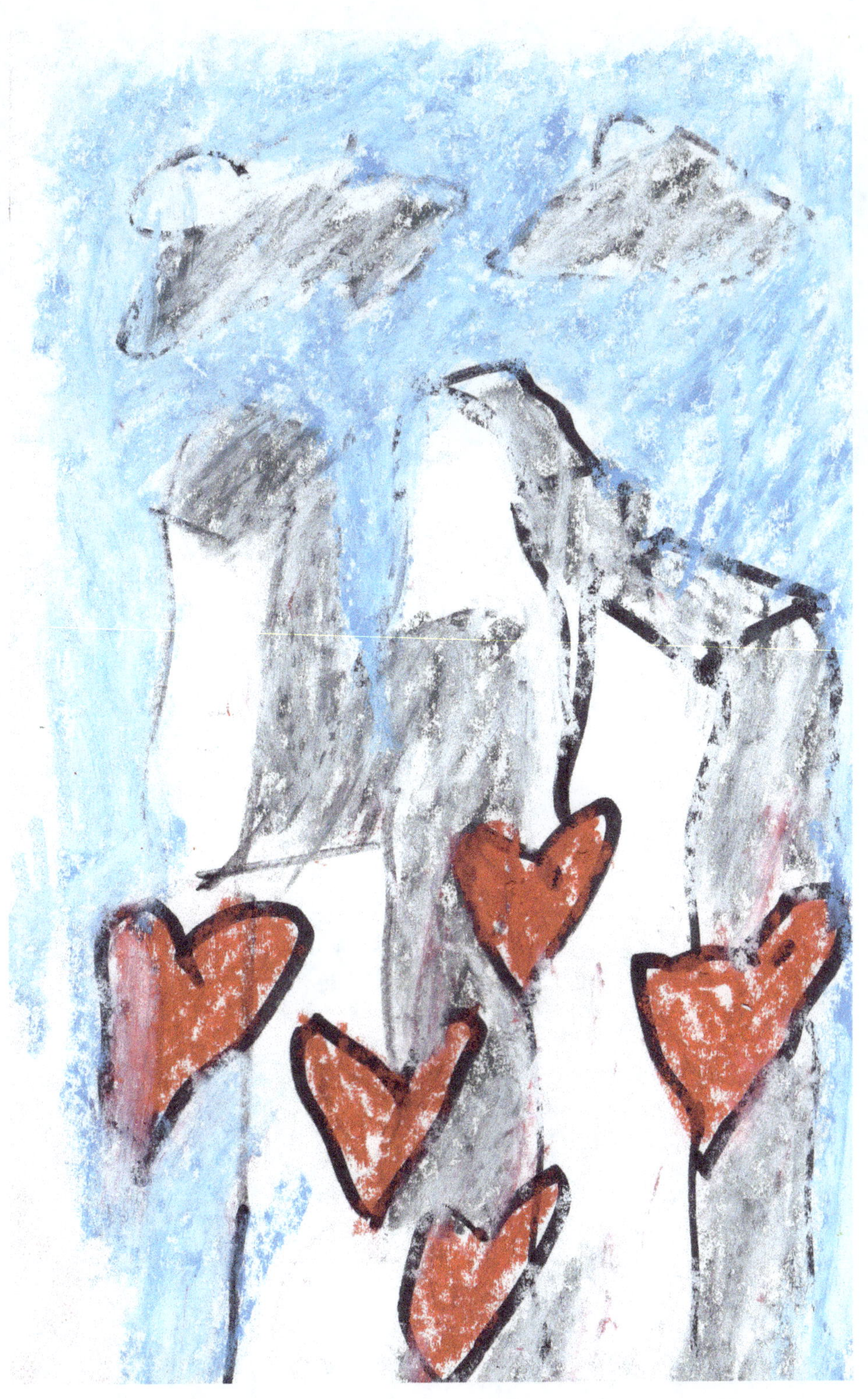

THE HEART LIVED
AMONGST MANY OTHER
HEARTS IN NYC
AMONGST SKYSCRAPERS
& FOREVER CHANGING
CLOUDS. IT WAS THE
PROUD OWNER OF A STURDY
PAIR OF SHOES & AN EXCELLENT
OVERCOAT

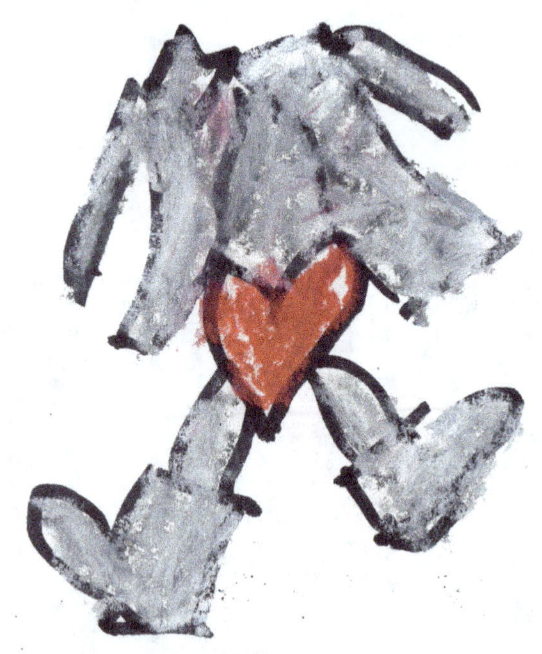

I WAS NOT AFRAID TO FACE
THE WEATHER RAIN OR SHINE
HAIL OR THUNDERSTORM

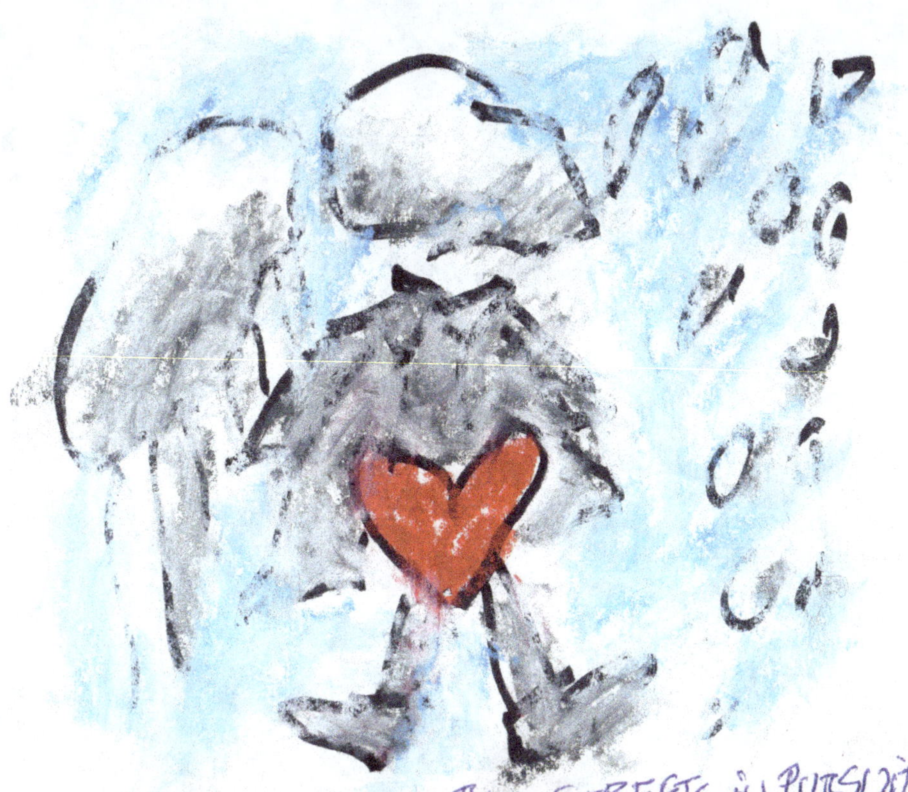

IT WALKED THE STREETS IN PURSUIT
OF DAILY CHORES LIKE OTHER HEARTS
WHETHER BORING OR INTERESTING

IT PATIENTLY WAITED FOR THE
GREEN LIGHT TO CROSS TO THE
OTHER SIDE + WHEN IT NOTICED
OLDER HEARTS INTIMIDATED BY
THE TRAFFIC IT GAVE THEM A HAND

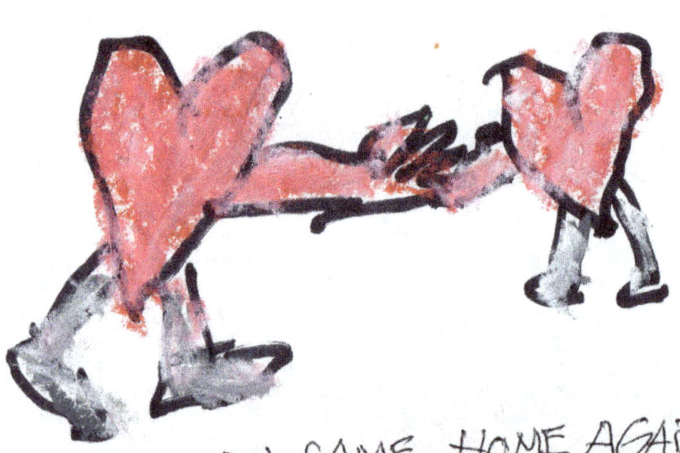

WHEN IT CAME HOME AGAIN
IT TOOK OFF ITS SHOES + WAS
BAREFOOT + ALONE

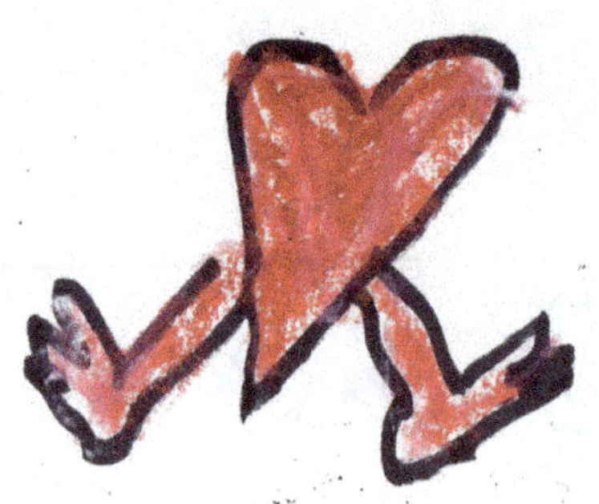

THEN IT TURNED ON THE RADIO
+ LISTENED TO THE GLIB VOICE OF
HEARTLESSNESS REPORTING ON
QUANTITIES OF DISTANT SUFFERING
WHICH MADE IT CRY + OPEN
THE WINDOW TO LOOK FOR CONSOLATION
IN THE SKY. BUT THE SKY DID
NOT TALK + WAS GREY + INDIFFERENT

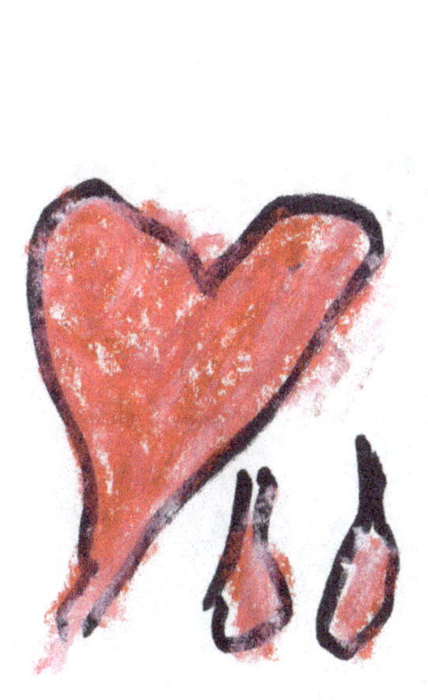

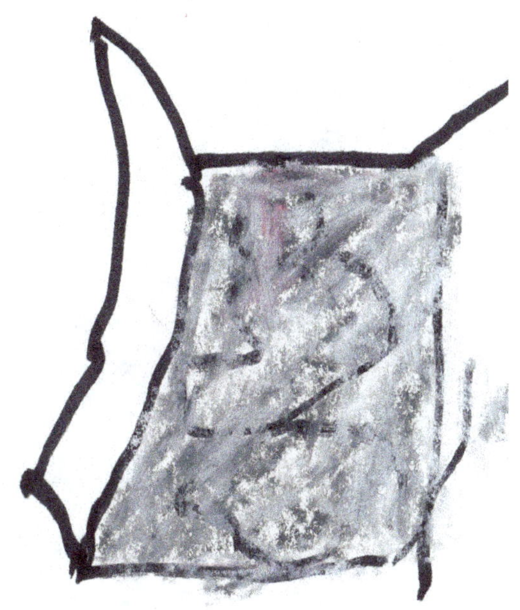

THEN ITS THROAT STARTED
THROBBING + IT WENT TO THE
DOCTOR FOR AN ANTI-THROBBING PILL

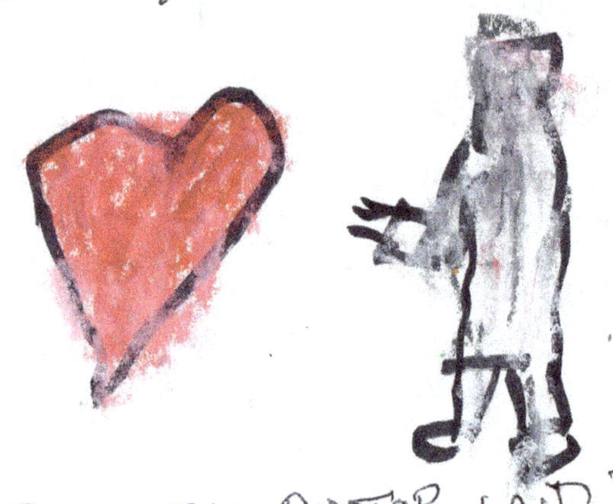

BUT THE DOCTOR SAID THERE IS
NO SUCH PILL
THEN IT WENT TO THE PHYSICAL
THERAPIST

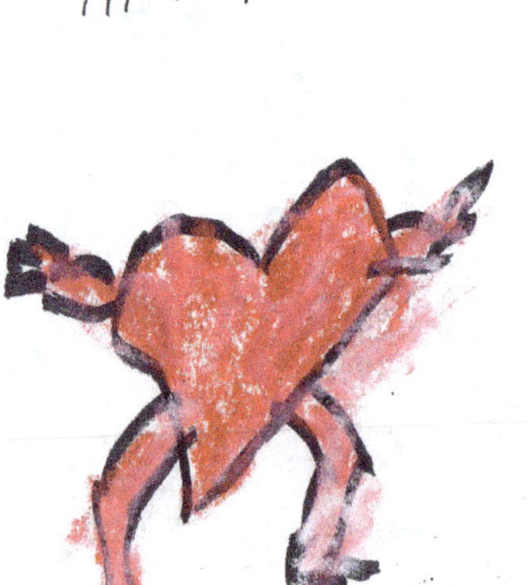

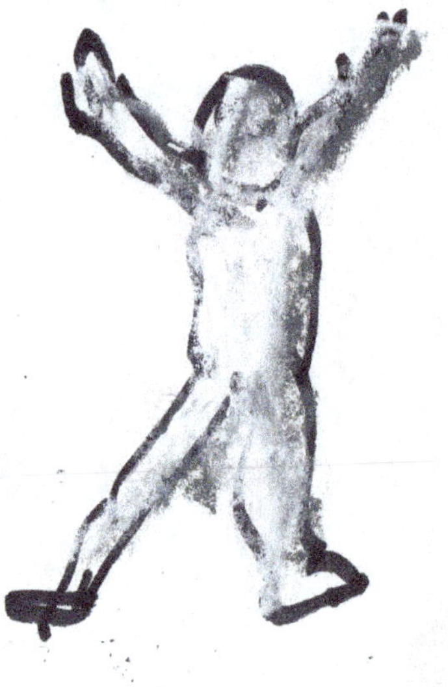

+ THAT DIDN'T WORK.
THEN IT REMEMBERED THERE
WAS A LOCAL MAGICIAN IN THE
NEIGHBORHOOD + IT WENT THERE
+ THE LOCAL MAGICIAN SAID:
THE THROBBING IS FROM THE
HEARTLESSNESS IN RESPONSE TO THE
QUANTITIES OF DISTANT SUFFERINGS
THERE IS ONLY ONE CURE FOR IT.
PUT ON YOUR SHOES + YOUR COAT
+ GO TILL YOU FIND THE DISTANT
SUFFERING. + WHEN YOU FIND IT
TAKE a DEEP BREATH

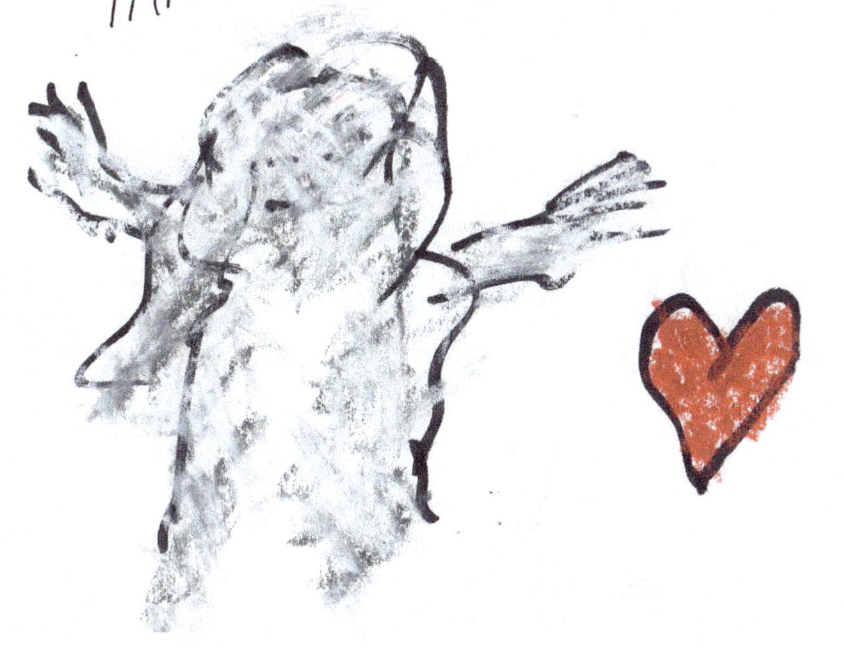

AND SAY

ABRA
KA
DABRA

TILL THE
SUFFERING
GOES AWAY

BREAD + PUPPET

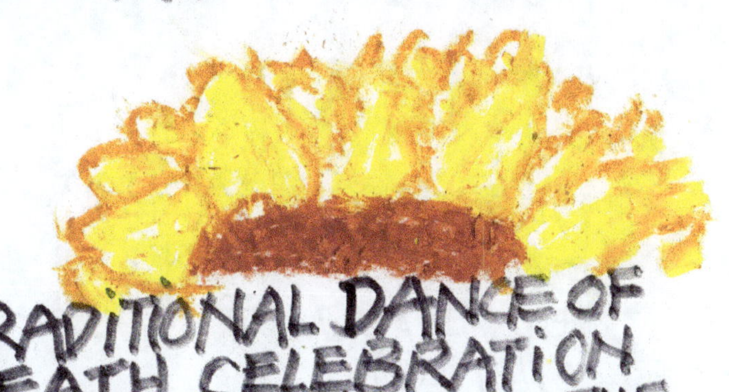

TRADITIONAL DANCE OF
DEATH CELEBRATION
FOR THE VICTIMS OF THE
ASSISTANT MASSMURDERER
U.S. SECRETARY OF STATE
ANTONY BLINKEN

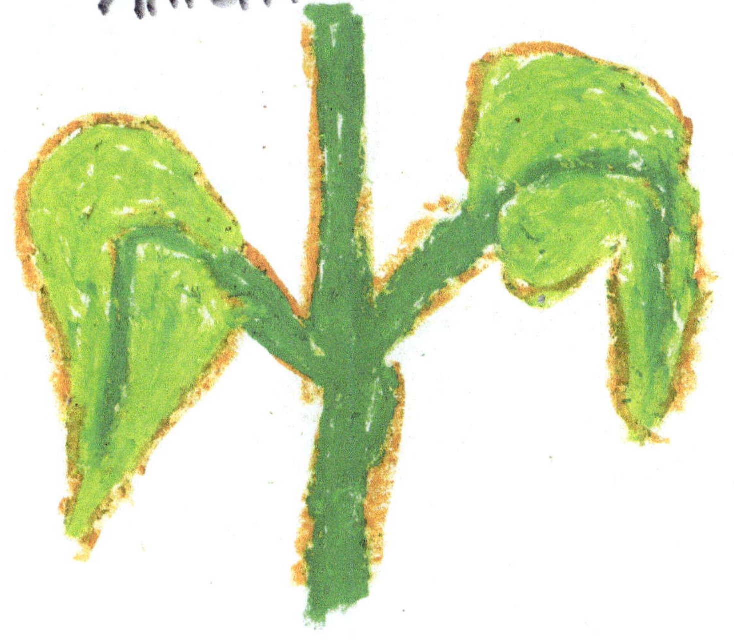

DR. TARIR HADDAD
DECLINED MEETING
SECRETARY OF STATE
BLINKEN

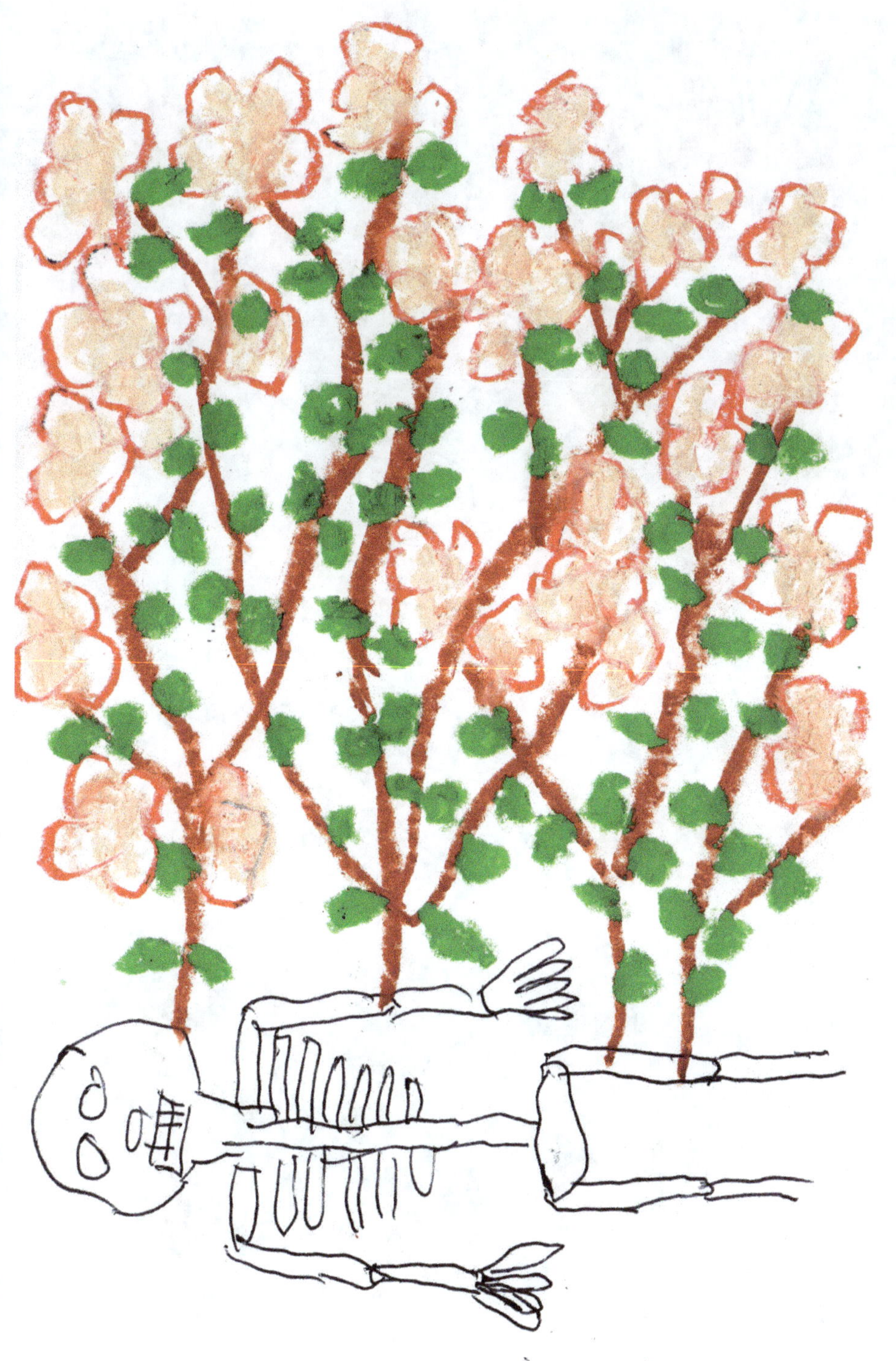

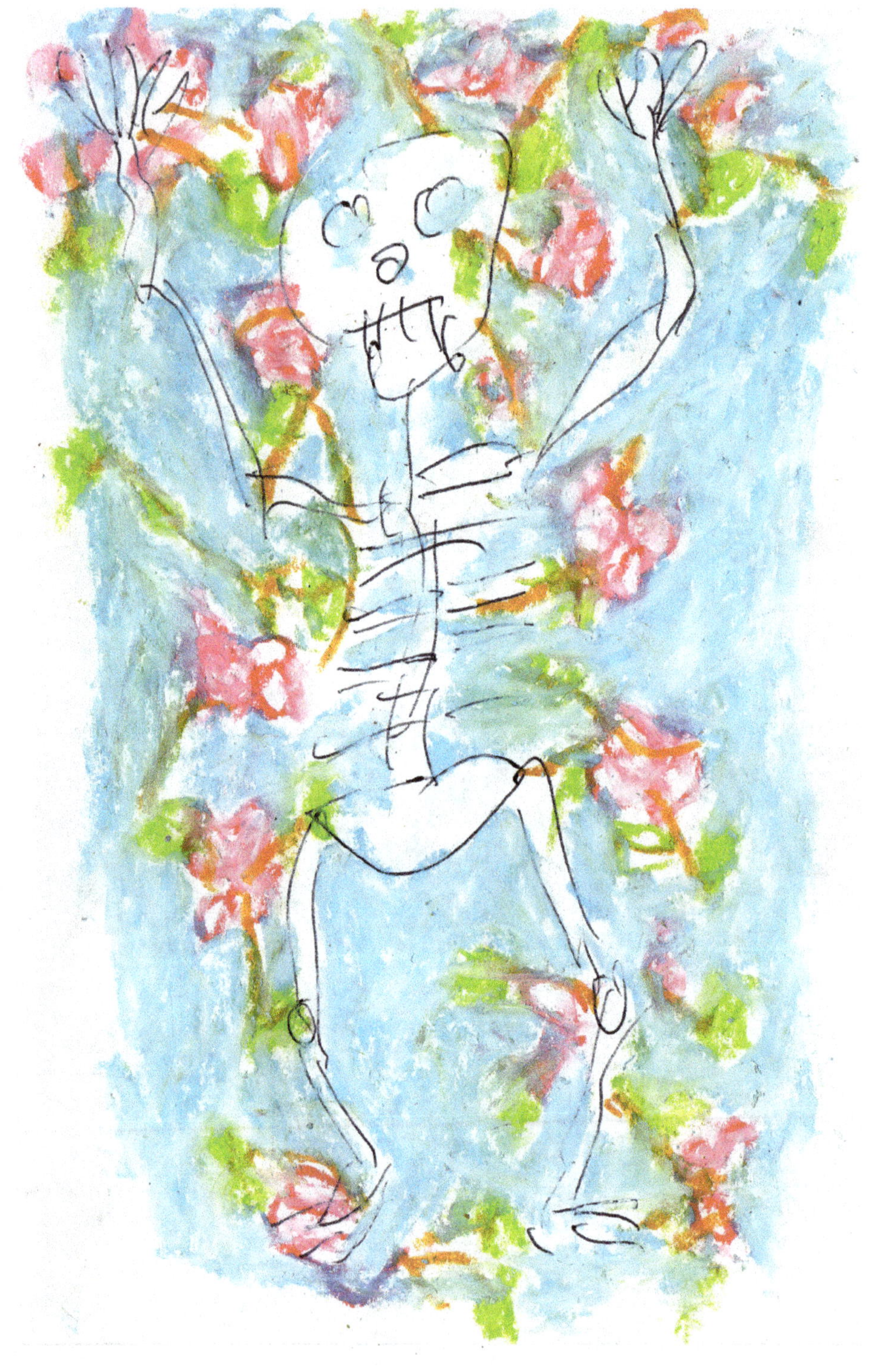

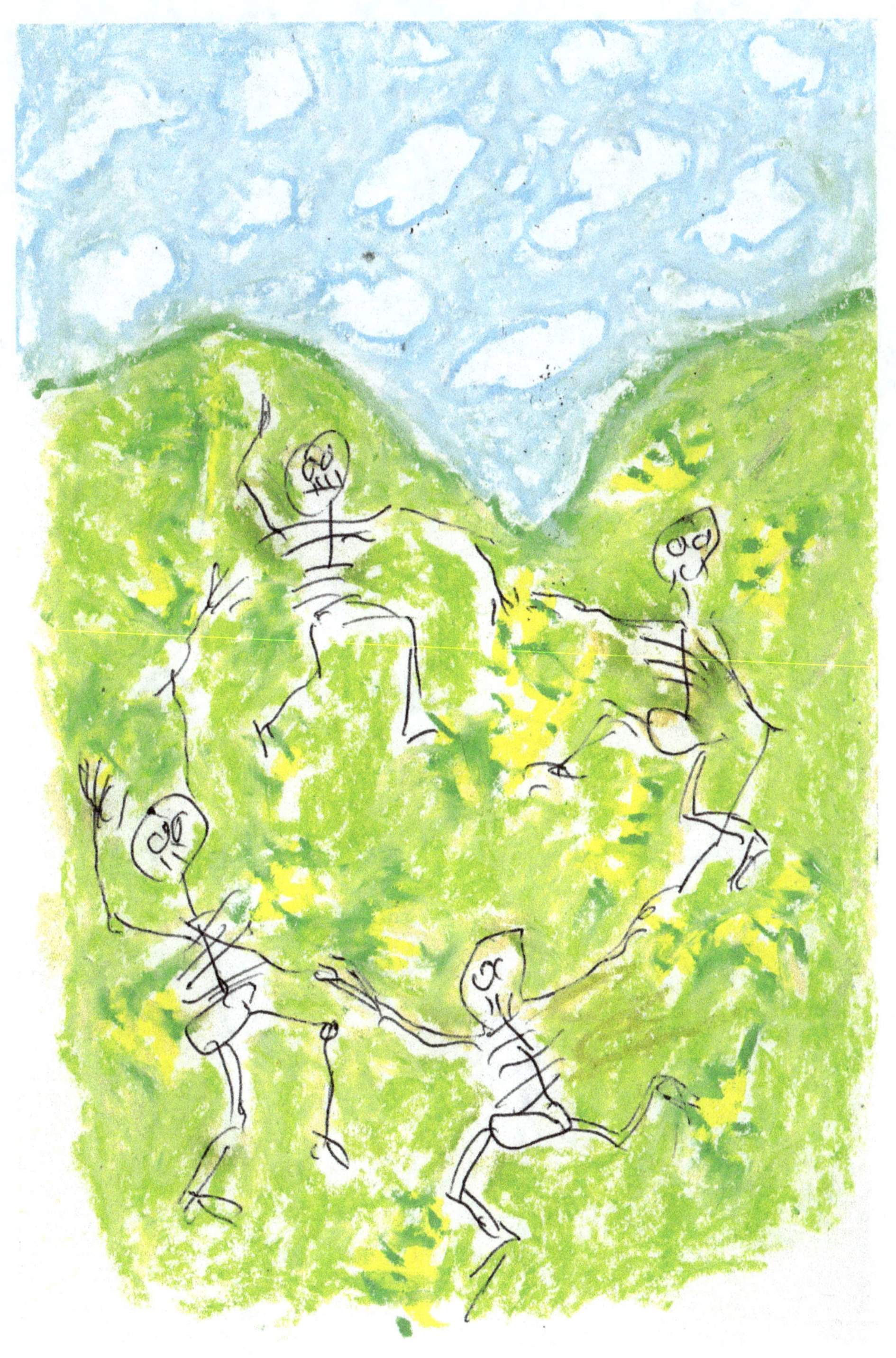

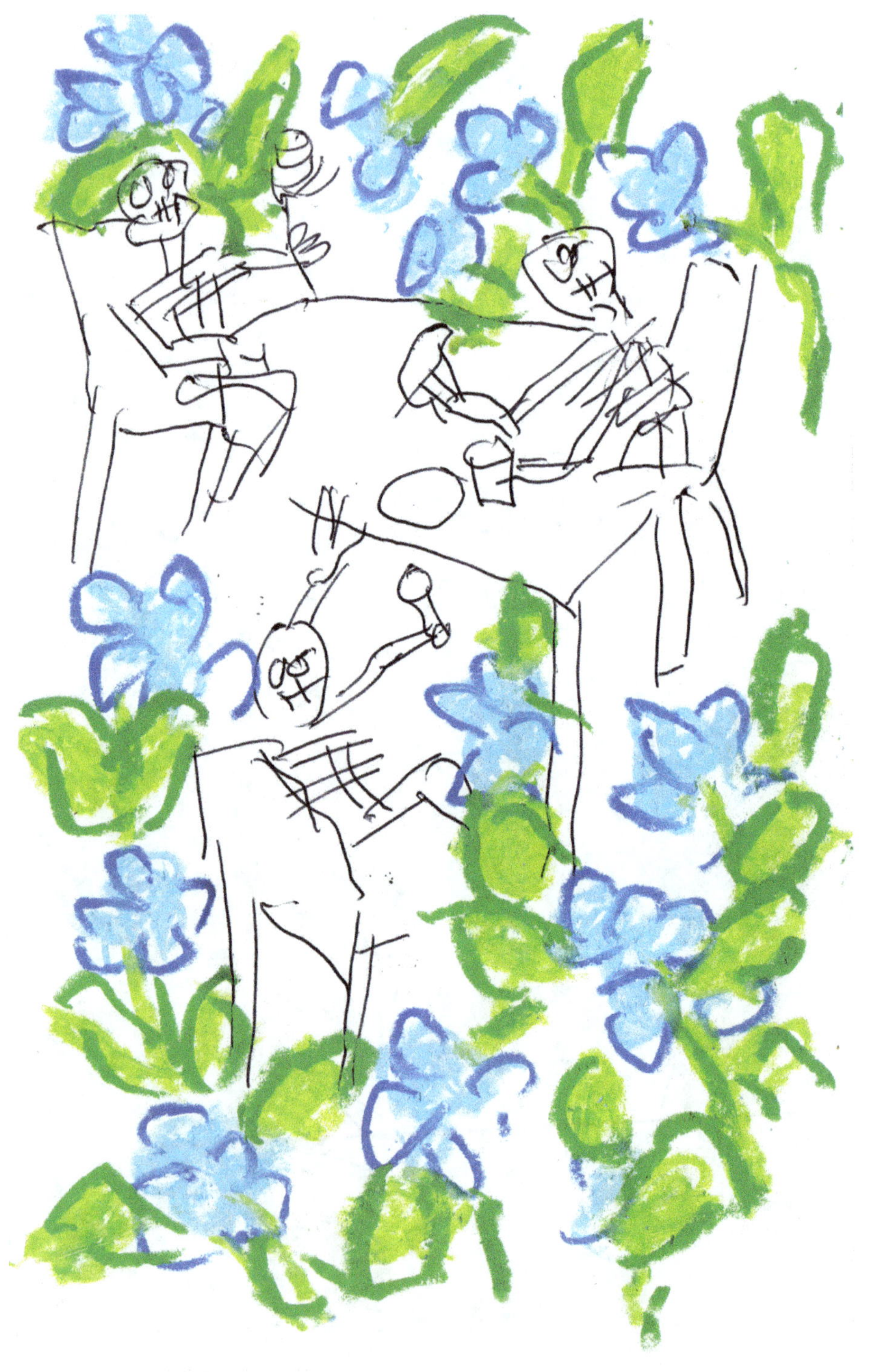

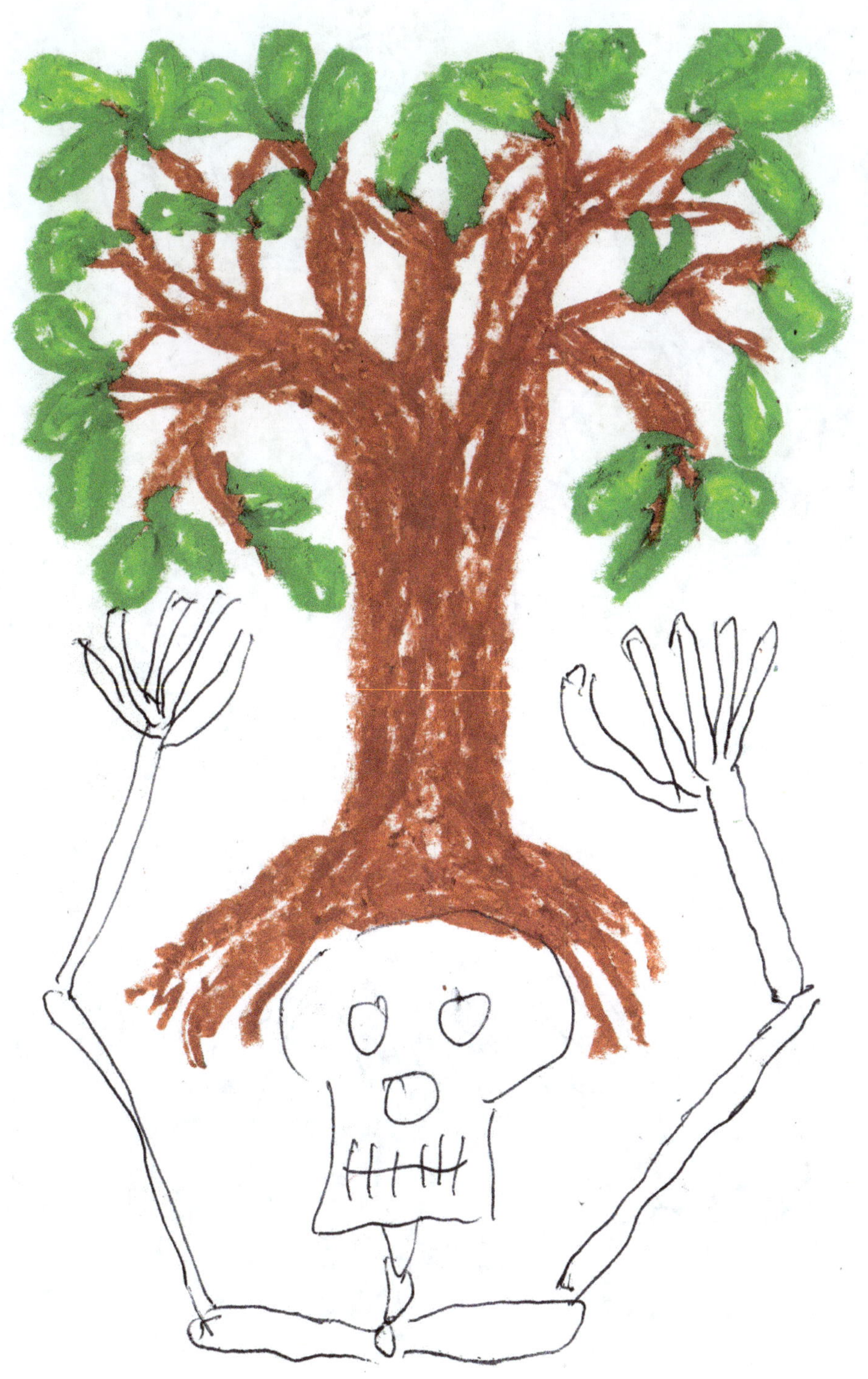

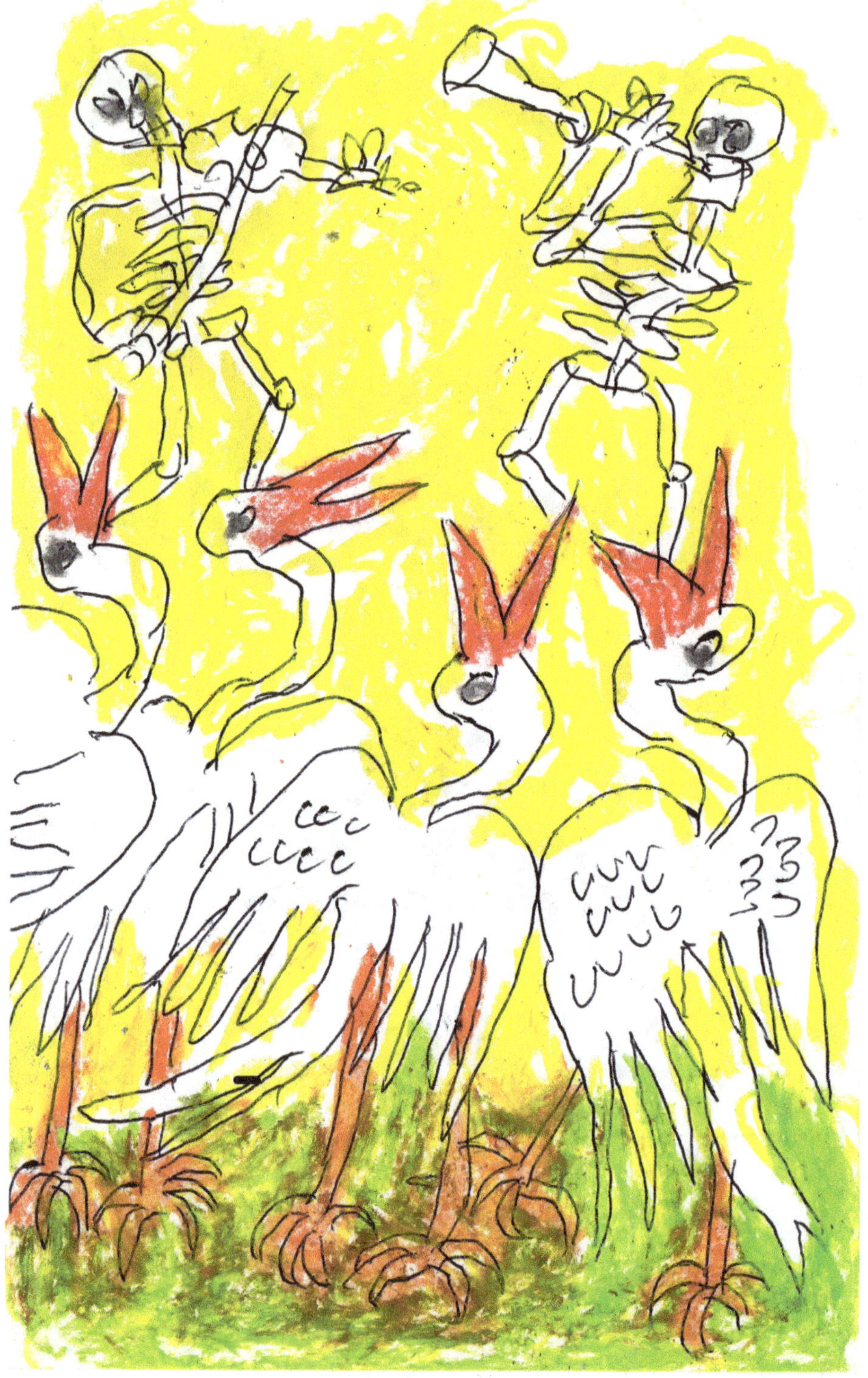

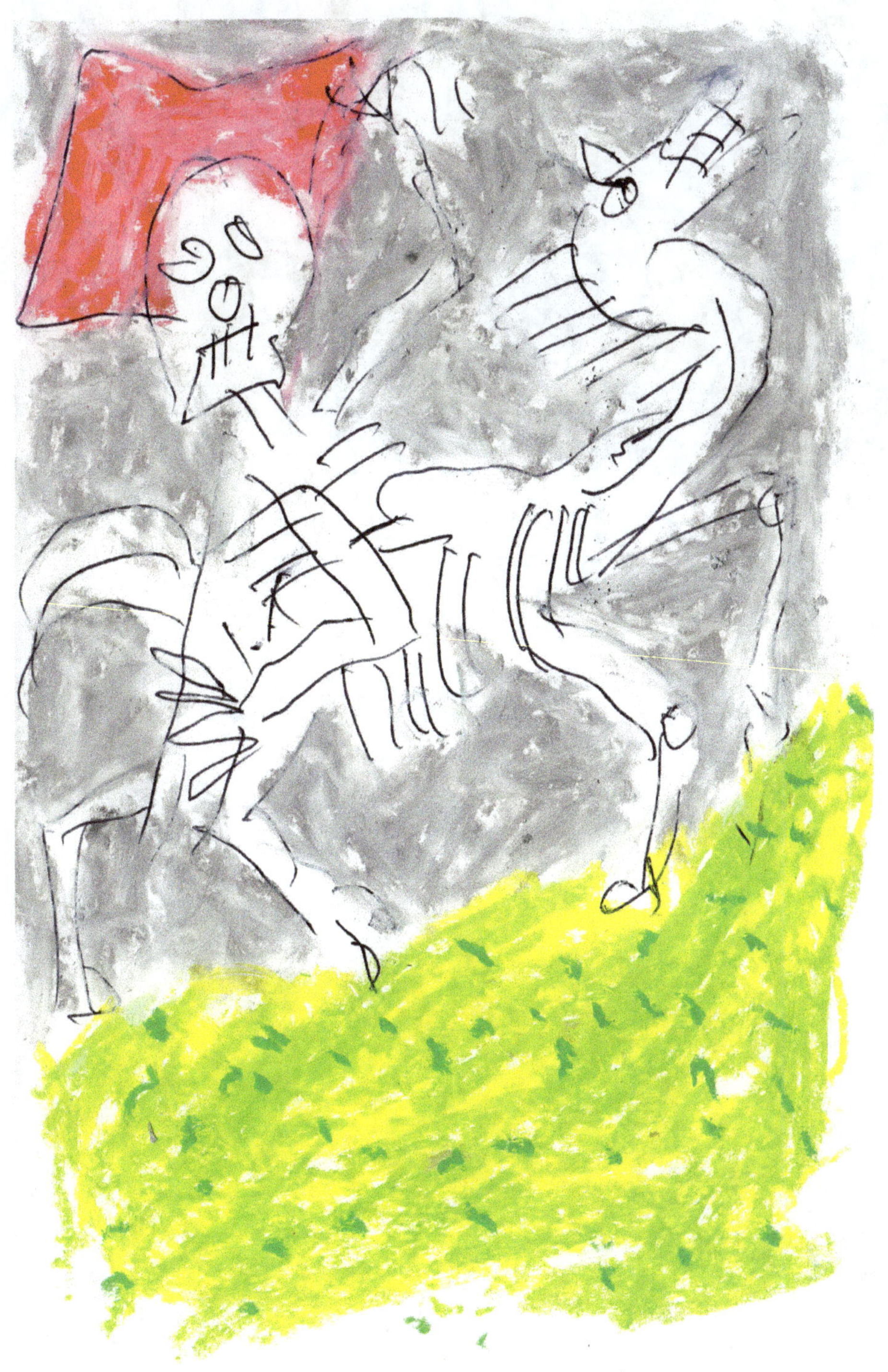

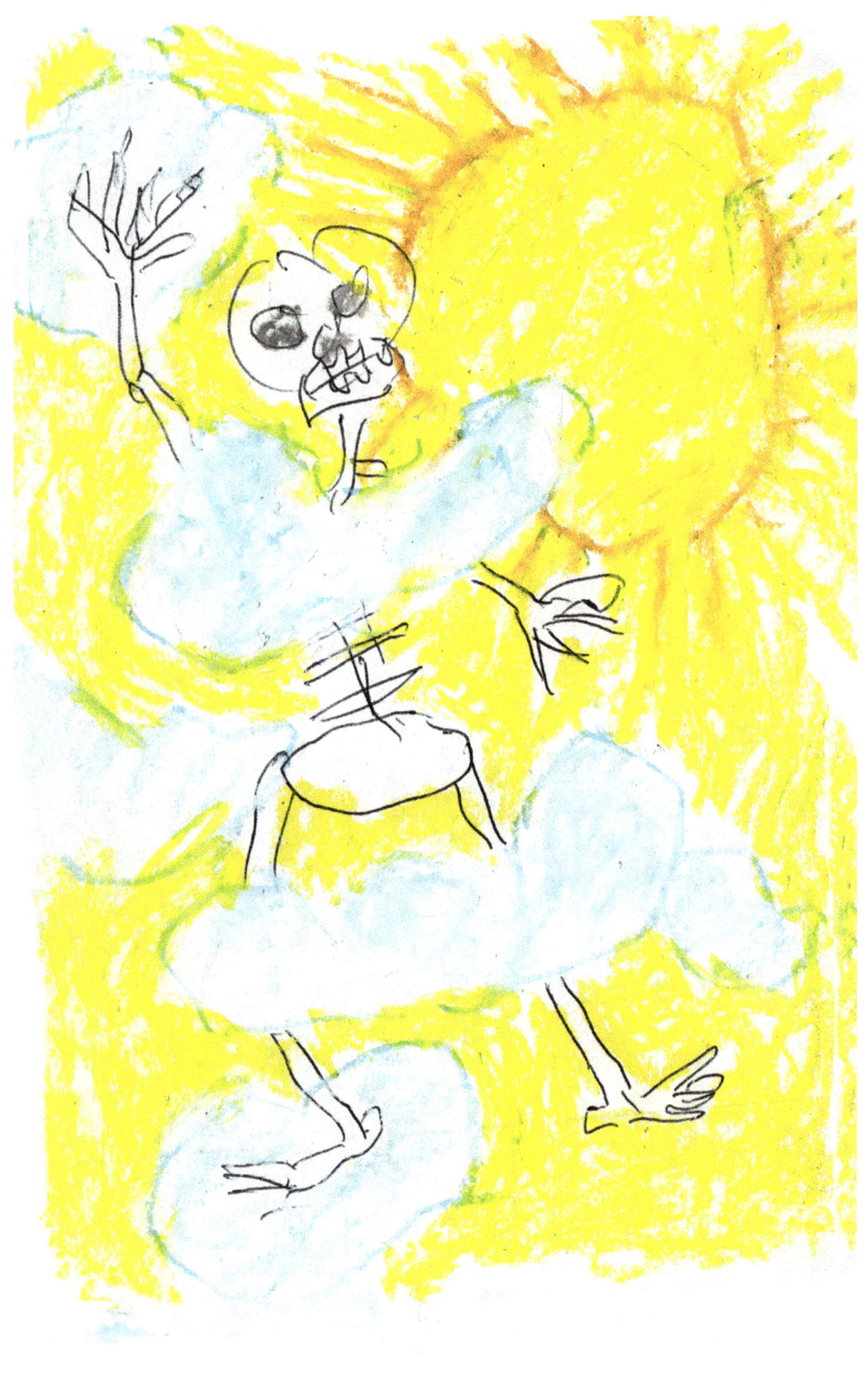

Order books from
https://breadandpuppetpress.org/collections/fomite-press

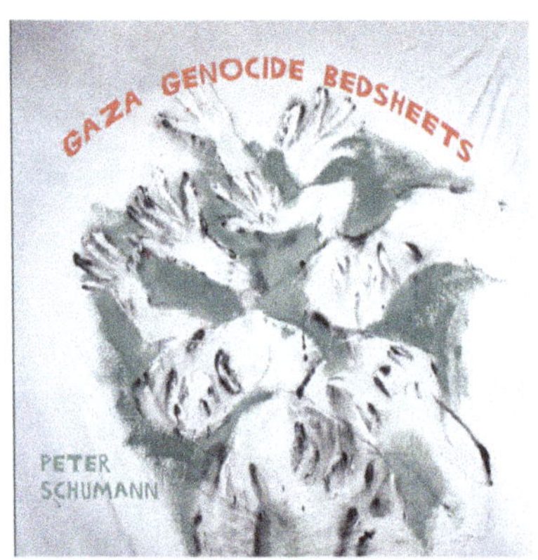

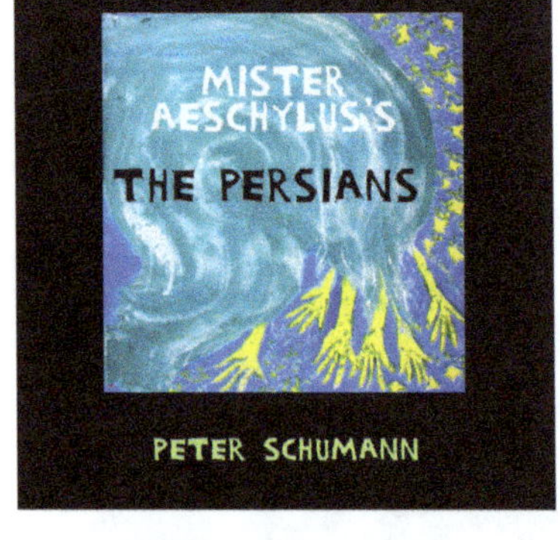

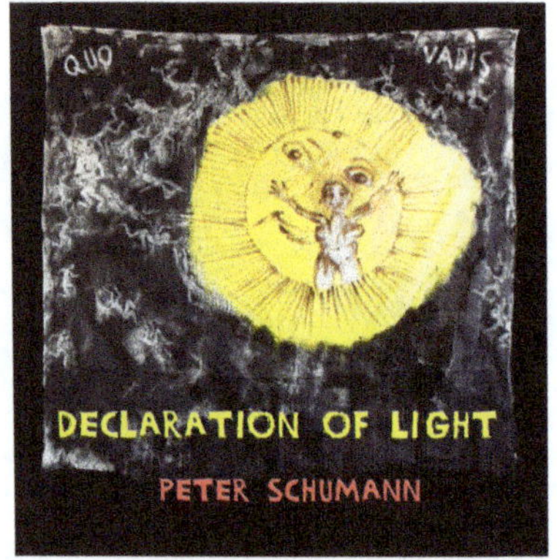

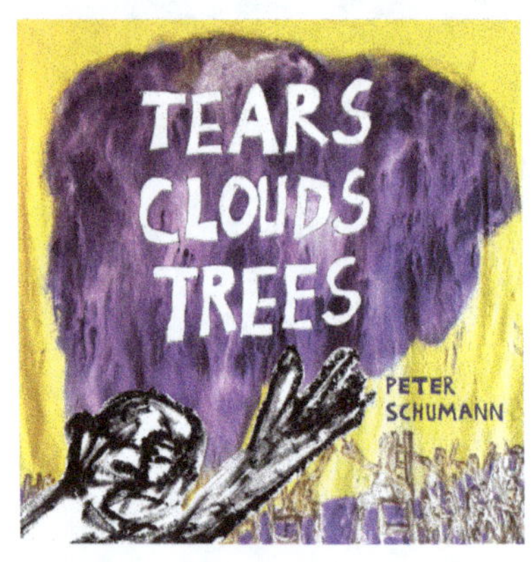

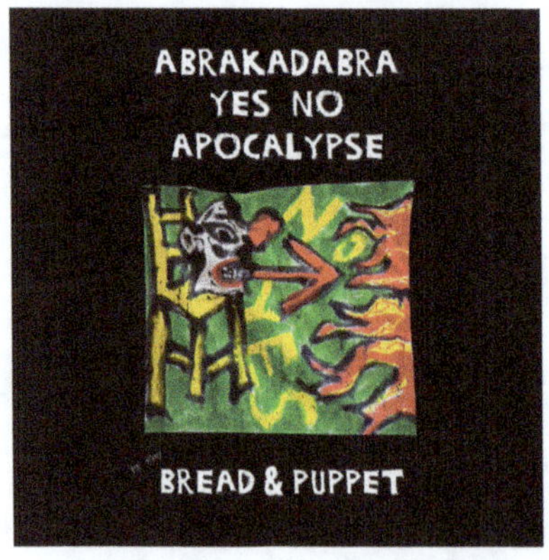

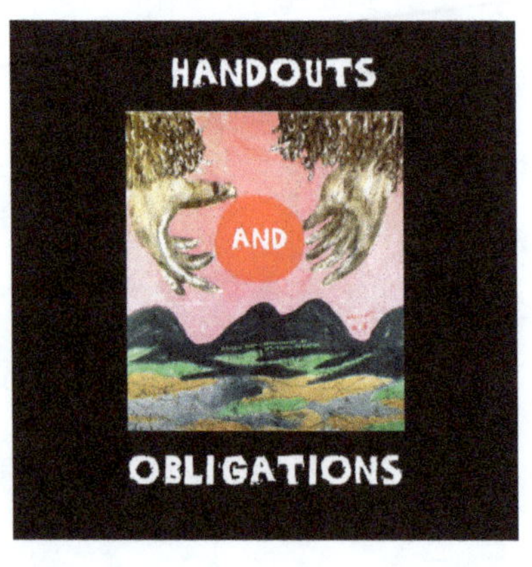

PETER SCHUMANN is the founder and
director of the Bread & Puppet Theater.
Born in Silesia, he was a sculptor and
dancer in Germany before moving to
the United States in 1961.

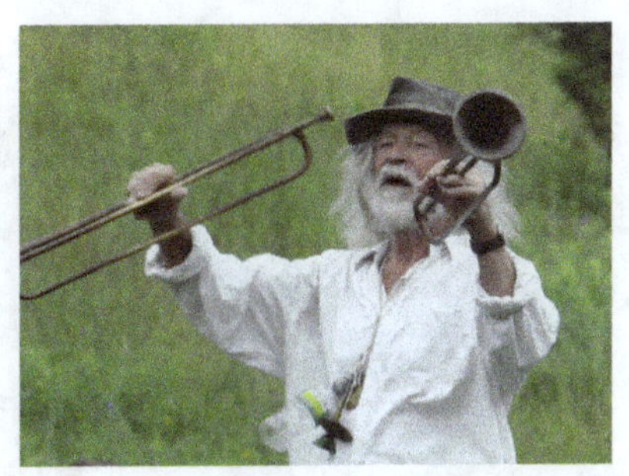

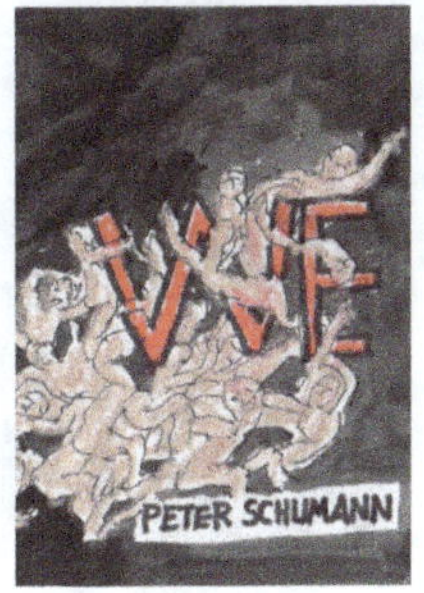

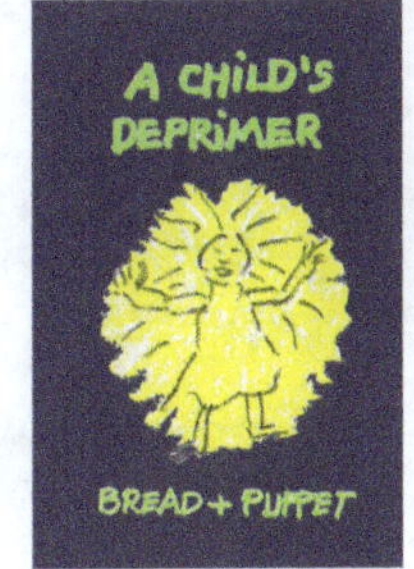

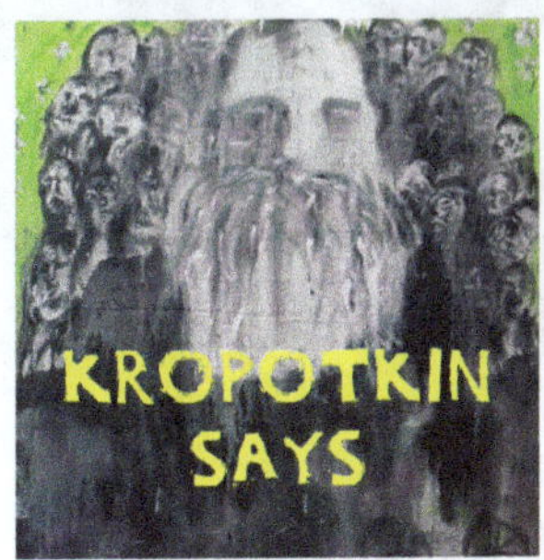

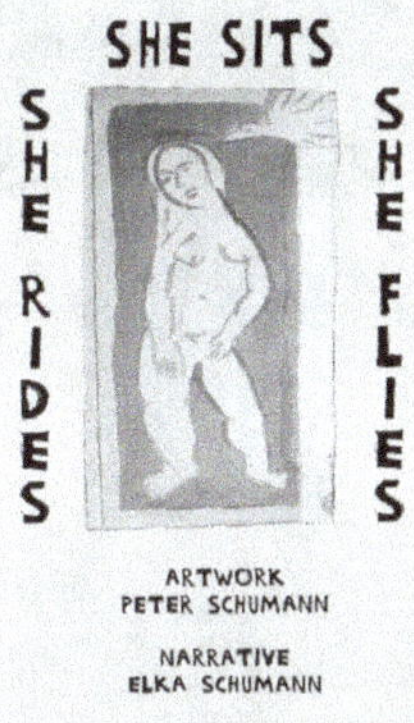

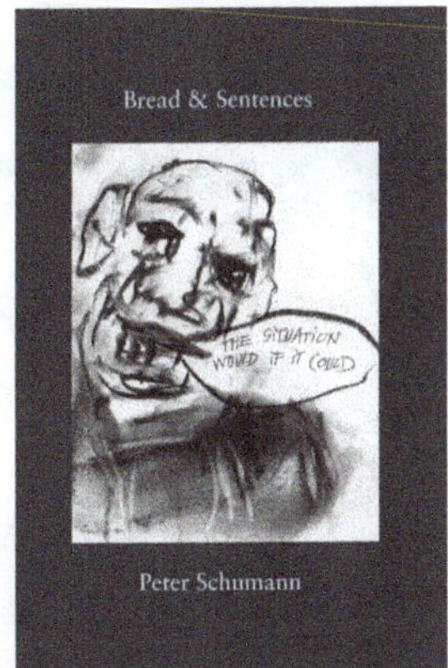

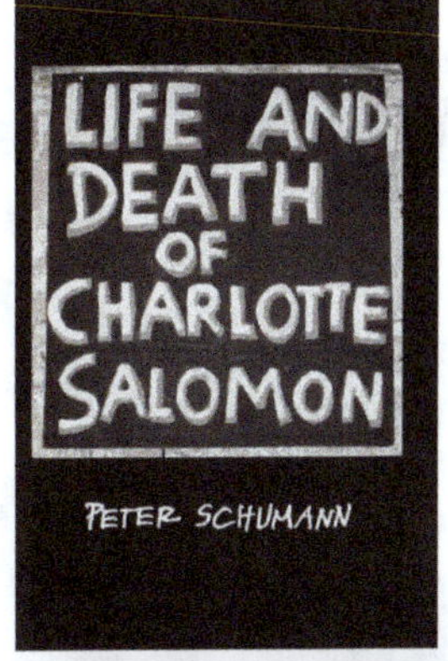

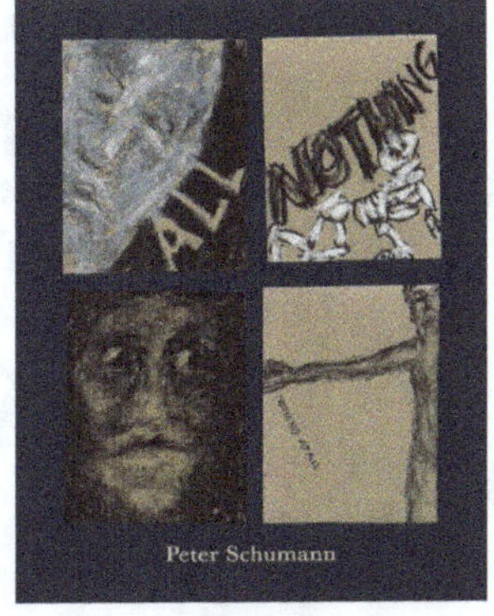

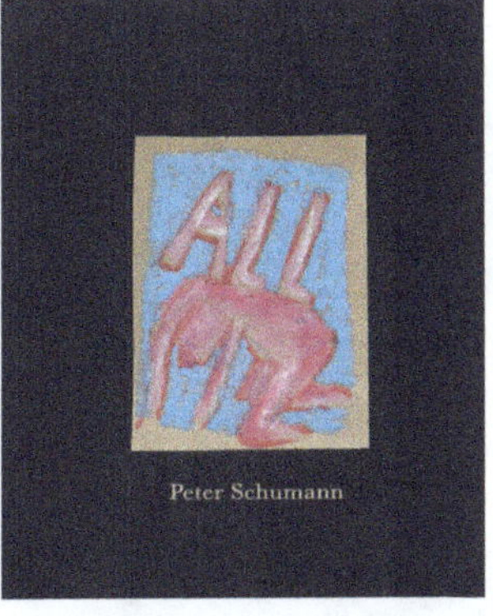

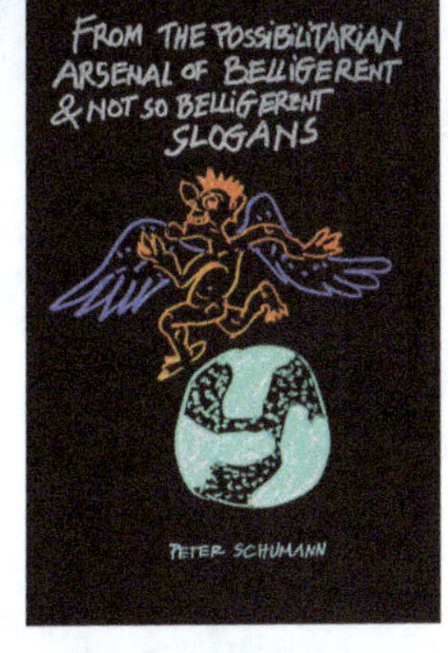

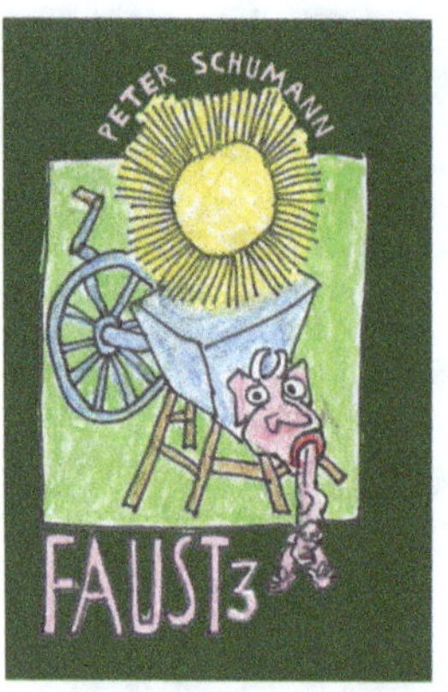

PETER SCHUMANN
FAUST3

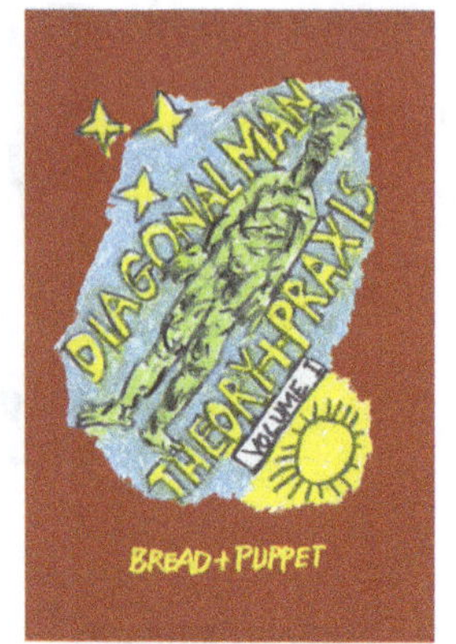

DIAGONAL MAN
THEORY+PRAXIS
VOLUME I
BREAD+PUPPET

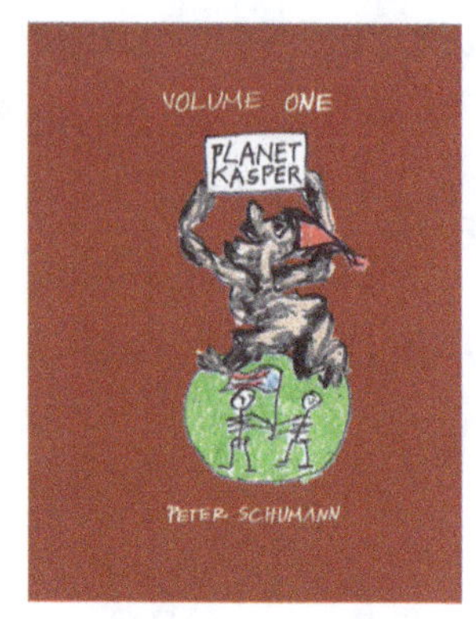

VOLUME ONE
PLANET KASPER
PETER SCHUMANN

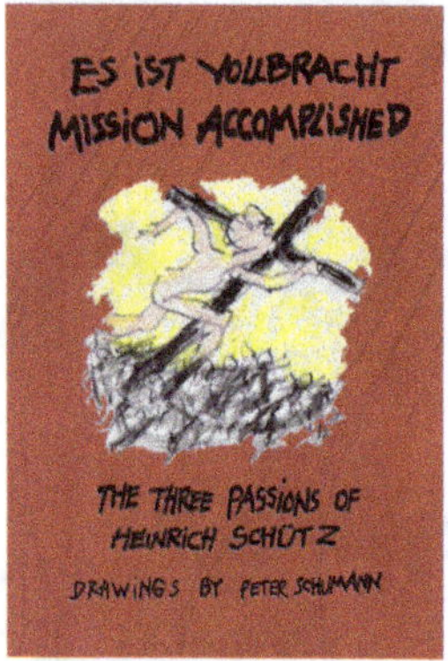

ES IST VOLLBRACHT
MISSION ACCOMPLISHED
THE THREE PASSIONS OF
HEINRICH SCHÜTZ
DRAWINGS BY PETER SCHUMANN

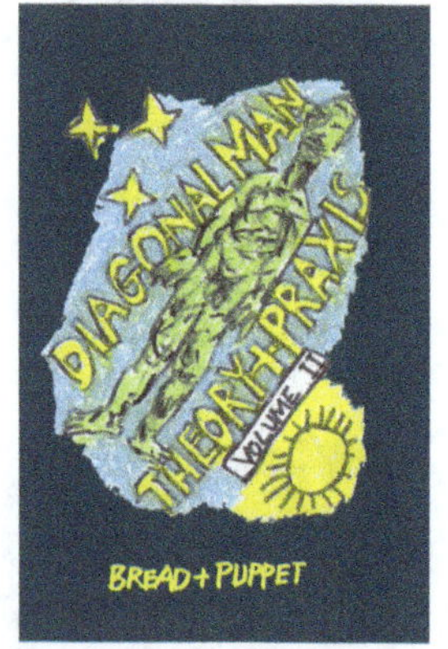

DIAGONAL MAN
THEORY+PRAXIS
VOLUME II
BREAD+PUPPET

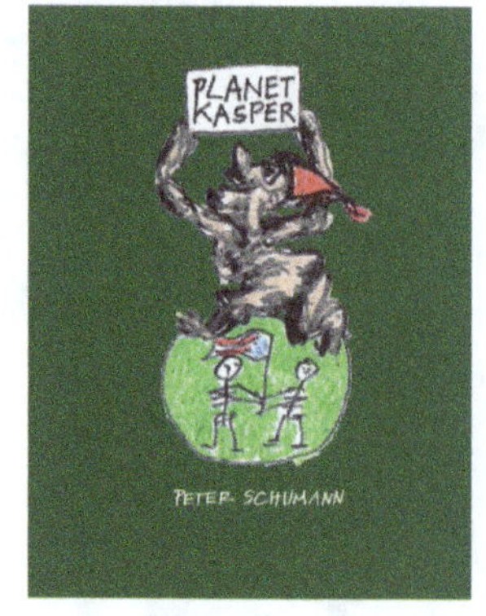

PLANET KASPER
PETER SCHUMANN

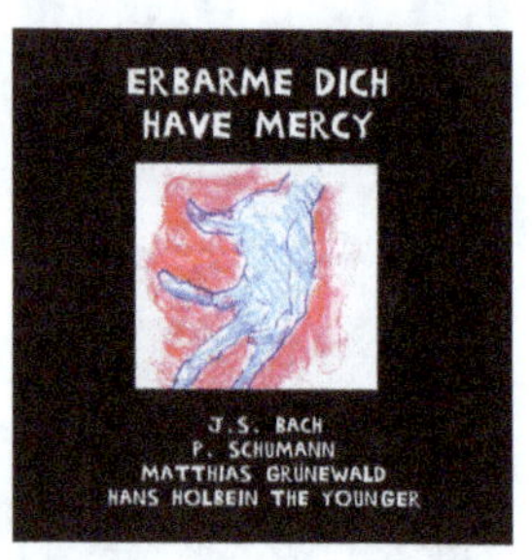

ERBARME DICH
HAVE MERCY
J.S. BACH
P. SCHUMANN
MATTHIAS GRÜNEWALD
HANS HOLBEIN THE YOUNGER

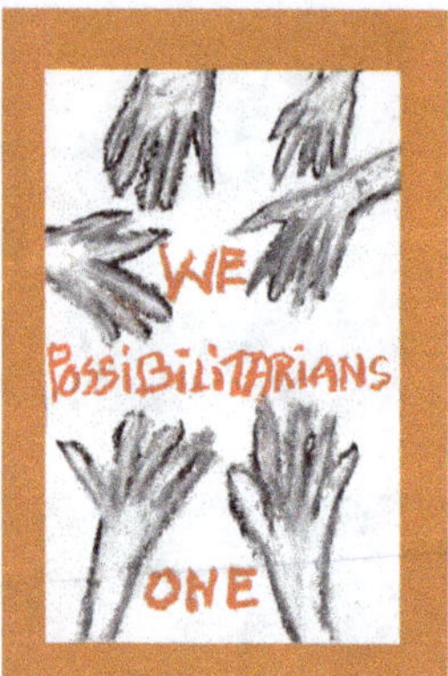

WE
POSSIBILITARIANS
ONE